The Railways of Upper Strathearn

Crieff-Balquhidder

by
Bernard Byrom

D1555847

THE OAKWOOD PRESS

© Oakwood Press & Bernard Byrom 2004

British Library Cataloguing in Publication Data
A Record for this book is available from the British Library
ISBN 0 85361 622 1

Typeset by Oakwood Graphics.
Repro by Ford Graphics, Ringwood, Hants.
Printed by Cambrian Printers Ltd, Aberystwyth, Ceredigion.

Above: Pickersgill class '113' 4-4-0 No. 54476 approaches Lochearnhead viaduct on 2nd June, 1951 with the 12.30 pm from Perth to Balquhidder. The line of trees high on the hillside mark the course of the Callander & Oban line as it descends from Glenoglehead to Balquhidder Junction.
H.C. Casserley

Title page: Pickersgill class '113' 4-4-0 No. 54476 awaits departure from Balquhidder with the 2.25 pm to Crieff. Although the photograph was taken on 2nd June, 1951 the noticeboard on the platform still bears the heading 'London Midland & Scottish Railway'.
H.C. Casserley

Front cover: St Fillans station in 1901 shortly after the line opened. An up (eastbound) train is standing at the down platform whilst passengers and staff pose for this official photograph. At that time St Fillans was the terminus of the line and it was not necessary for the normal timetabled passenger trains to use the island platform.
National Railway Museum/STR 388
Rear cover, top: A Caledonian Railway postcard of Lochearnhead station. The magnificent nine-arch viaduct in the background carried the line across the southern approach to Glen Ogle and was built entirely of concrete.
John Alsop Collection
Rear cover, bottom: A period postcard of Balquhidder station with the canopy over the station's subway prominent in front of the station building.
John Alsop Collection

Published by The Oakwood Press (Usk), P.O. Box 13, Usk, Mon., NP15 1YS.
E-mail: oakwood-press@dial.pipex.com
Website: www.oakwood-press.dial.pipex.com

Contents

A Pickersgill class '72' 4-4-0 with a badly scorched smokebox door lifts a Crieff-bound train out of Lochearnhead in 1950. The line of trees on the hillside marks the course of the Callander & Oban line as it climbs Glen Ogle.   *R.D. Stephen*

Railways around Crieff

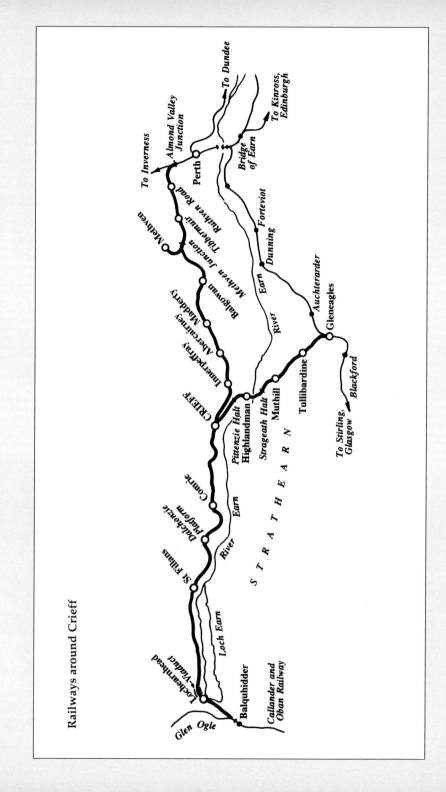

Bibliography and Acknowledgements

The material for this book has come partly from the author's fairly extensive knowledge of railway history, extending back over more than half a century of study, and partly from the following sources:

Primary Sources

Colonel Williamson's Papers relating to the Crieff & Comrie Railway (Perth & Kinross Council Archives at the A.K. Bell Library, Perth, Reference MS84)

Articles and reports in the *Strathearn Herald*, *Perthshire Advertiser* and *Perthshire Courier* (Local History section, A.K. Bell Library, Perth)

Caledonian Railway Minute Books (National Archives of Scotland, Edinburgh, Series Reference BR/CAL)

Caledonian Railway Register House Plans (National Archives of Scotland, Edinburgh, Series Reference RHP)

Caledonian Railway Working and Public Timetables (National Archives of Scotland)

National Railway Museum, York (Photographic Archives)

Crieff & Comrie Railway Prospectuses 1880 and 1889 (Perth & Kinross Archives, MS84)

Evidence to the House of Commons Select Committee (Perth & Kinross Archives, MS84)

Crieff & Comrie Railway Act 1890 (Perth & Kinross Archives, MS84)

Lochearnhead, St Fillans & Comrie Railway Act 1897 (Perth & Kinross Archives, MS84)

George Mackay & Son v Crieff & Comrie Railway Company - Court of Session, 19/7/1894 - evidence to Lord Low (Perth & Kinross Archives, MS84)

Secondary Sources

The History of Crieff (Alexander Porteous, 1912)

Annals of St Fillans (Alexander Porteous, 1912)

'Development of the Caledonian Railway in 1901' (*Railway Magazine*, December 1901)

'From East to West in Central Scotland' (*Railway Magazine*, August 1904)

'The new Caledonian Railway belt across Scotland' (*Transport & Railroad Gazette*, 12th May, 1905)

'Comrie & Lochearnhead Railway' (*The Locomotive Magazine*, 15th August, 1905)

'1935 Excursion to St Fillans' (Robert H. Drummond, publication not known)

'Last Days of the Balquhidder - Comrie Line' (George Robin, publication not known)

The True Line (Journals of the Caledonian Railway Association)

The Callander & Oban Railway (re Balquhidder Junction - John Thomas 1972)

'The Railways of Crieff' (*Steam Days*, June 1997)

Acknowledgements

The author's thanks are also due to the following individuals, in alphabetical order, who have provided material, photographs and memories of the lines:

Mr & Mrs P. Burnell (Corbridge)
Mrs A. Cameron (Comrie)
Mr D. Campbell (Crieff)
Mr & Mrs J. Carmichael (Comrie)
Mr G. Doig (Henley-on-Thames)
Mr W. Gardiner (Comrie)
Mr C. Grant (Forfar)
Mr J. McEwan (Comrie)

Miss J. MacGregor (Comrie)
Mr J.D. MacIntosh (Caledonian Railway Association)
Mr E. McNab (Portlethen)
Ms C. Miller (Comrie)
Mr R. Munro (Comrie)
Mr J. Scott Miller, Pittachar (Crieff)
Mrs E. Wilson and Mr J. Wilson (Comrie)

and also Mr Steve Connelly, Archivist, Mr Jeremy Duncan, Local Studies Librarian and their respective staffs at the A.K. Bell Library, Perth, for their patience and support in this project.

Introduction

In the 21st century, when a journey by motor car along the A85 from Comrie to Crieff occupies a mere 10 minutes, it is difficult to imagine the tremendous enthusiasm with which the people of Comrie welcomed the arrival in 1893 of the branch line from Crieff.

Comrie had been steadily increasing in size and prosperity in the second half of the 19th century but still depended on stagecoaches and general carriers for communication with the outside world. Wealthy people either rode on horseback or maintained their own carriages whilst the poorer people (of whom there were many) were accustomed to a two hour walk to Crieff.

This book tells of the efforts made over many decades to bring the railway from Crieff to Comrie and westwards to the shores of Loch Earn. Most of these efforts came to nothing but, in the end, it was the single-minded determination of one man above all others that achieved that goal.

That man was Colonel David Robertson Williamson, the Laird of Lawers, who eventually overcame all opposition and financial difficulties and succeeded in connecting Comrie with the national rail network. When the House of Commons passed the Crieff & Comrie Railway Act in 1890 the village went wild with excitement. Shortly after the line was opened in 1893 the village again went *en fête* and showed its gratitude by organising a public banquet and presentation in his honour.

Nowadays not even the opening of a new motorway or a much-needed bypass around a town arouses such local enthusiasm!

In 1905 the line was completed westwards to Balquhidder where it joined the Callander & Oban Railway. Its promoters had great hopes of Oban being developed as a major transatlantic port through which both passengers and merchandise, especially livestock, would travel by their line to Perth, Dundee and the north-east of Scotland instead of by the longer route via Callander and Dunblane. But it was not to be.

The line never really prospered in spite of attempts in the 1930s to develop it as a tourist route. By this time the motor car and charabanc were taking an increasing share of this traffic and this trend was accelerated after World War II. Moreover, just as the coming of railways had put an end to the old drove roads over which herds of cattle were driven over the moors to trysts in Crieff and later Falkirk, so the development of refrigerated container lorries largely put an end to long cattle trains on the railways.

The end came in 1951 for the Balquhidder-Comrie section of the line, and Comrie lost its rail service completely in 1964 when the remaining section to Crieff and Gleneagles was also closed.

In researching the book I have not only used original material held in the County Archives in Perth and in the National Archives of Scotland in Edinburgh but also quoted extensively from contemporary newspapers reports, principally those in the *Strathearn Herald*. In writing this account of the building, operation and eventual closure of the line I have attempted to strike a balance between the interests of the local and social historians as well as the railway enthusiast. These reports, although they may not always be accurate in all their details, vividly convey the excitement generated in a village whose transport system had been confined to the speed of a stagecoach or a horse-drawn cart and was now entering the modern age of steam transport.

And this was little more than a century ago!

Chapter One

Before the Railways Came

For many centuries the roads in Strathearn, in common with most of Britain, were little better than cart tracks. Generally, the only roads in Scotland worthy of their name were the military roads constructed by General Wade for the rapid deployment of Government troops after the Jacobite defeat at Culloden in 1746.

An Act of Parliament of 1669 had dealt with the building and repairing of highways and bridges. Under this Act, every able-bodied man was required to give six days labour yearly to help build or improve the roads in his parish. The Act stated that 'all tenants and cottars and their servants . . . should have in readiness horses, carts, sleds, spades, shovels, picks, mattocks and other such instruments as shall be required for repairing said highways'. Fines were imposed on anyone who refused to carry out this duty.

These 'Parish Road Days', as they were known, were very unpopular and the standard of workmanship was indifferent, to say the least. The villagers usually did their work grudgingly and inefficiently and, because their surveyors and overseers were usually appointed because of their local standing rather than their expertise, it was often found that a combination of ill-directed labour, inexperience and bad weather combined to leave the roads in a worse state than ever.

This system was superseded by the Turnpike Act of 1751 which levied a yearly assessment of 1s. 6d. on every male over 18 years of age. 'Turnpike Trusts' were set up to build and maintain decent roads but the traveller had to pay tolls to travel over them. Toll bars were set up at each end of a Trust's road and an adjacent toll-house, manned by a toll-keeper, was built at which the tolls were collected.

Not surprisingly, travellers resented having to pay tolls and there was universal satisfaction when the system was abolished in 1878 and responsibility for roads was transferred to District Councils.

The original road from Crieff to Comrie and the west went down past Milnab, crossed the Bridge of Turret and continued via Laggan and Strowan where it crossed the Earn on an old stone bridge which later plays an important part in our story.

The present main road between Crieff and Comrie was a toll road that was built in 1804, a toll-house being situated by the new bridge at Dalvreck. This bridge was widened in 1889. The toll-house at the Comrie end was situated in Drummond Street near Melville Square.

Following the improvements brought about by turnpike roads, the first public coach between Crieff and Comrie began running in April 1859. Its official name was 'The Strathearn Lass' but it was colloquially known as the 'Comrie Dasher' and it ran until the railway to Comrie was opened in 1893.

In 1865 another coach called 'The Prince Charlie' began running between Crieff, Comrie and St Fillans. It was not a commercial success and the service was soon discontinued.

In 1872 the Caledonian Railway Company inaugurated a once-daily coach service between its stations at Crieff and Lochearnhead. When the railway was opened to Comrie in 1893 the coach service started from there but the extension of the railway to Balquhidder in 1905 finally put an end to coach services in Upper Strathearn.

Attempts had also been made in earlier days to improve communications by means of building a navigable canal from Perth to Loch Earn. Such a proposal had been made as early as 1793 by James Drummond of Comrie, who suggested a canal four feet deep and eight feet wide. A later survey was made in 1819 by Robert Stevenson, better known for his construction of lighthouses and harbours but, once again, nothing came of the idea.

James Drummond had suggested the canal should be linked at Comrie with a turnpike road running from Stirling via Dunblane, Glenlichorn and Glenlednock to Loch Tay, thus opening up a countryside containing upwards of 100,000 people.

In those days, the glens such as Glenartney and Glenlednock were quite densely populated with crofters and smallholders. Many of these were eking out a bare living and one of the objectives of the canal's promoters was to encourage these crofters to move to newly erected villages along the line of the canal where they could develop the woollen industry.

This grand design came to nothing. However, around 1830, a turnpike road (now the B827) was constructed over the moors from Braco to Comrie. One toll-house was situated where the road branches from the A822 just north of Braco and the other was built near Cultybraggan where the long straight stretch of road from Dalginross takes a sharp right-hand bend.

The proposed extension of the road northwards over the hills to Loch Tay never materialised. The road up Glenlednock was improved but, from Invergeldie at the head of the glen to Loch Tay, there are only the remains of the ancient drove road.

Before the railways came to Upper Strathearn: the Caledonian Railway Company's connecting road coach c.1890, outside the Royal Hotel at Comrie.

Chapter Two

Origins of the Crieff & Comrie Railway

Railways first reached Perth on 22nd May, 1848 when the Scottish Central Railway arrived from the South via Stirling.

The line was engineered by Joseph Locke who, together with Robert Stephenson and Isambard Kingdom Brunel, was one of the great triumvirate of railway builders of the mid-19th century. He had already built practically the whole of the main line railway between Birmingham and Glasgow via Lancaster and Carlisle, over the summits of Shap and Beattock, as well as many hundreds of miles of railways on the continent. In Scotland he also engineered the Scottish Midland Junction Railway's line between Perth and Forfar and the Glasgow, Paisley & Greenock Railway.

However, both these Scottish railways were too small to survive for long as independent companies. Before long they were both absorbed by the mighty Caledonian Railway as part of their Carlisle-Glasgow-Aberdeen network.

Railway competition was fierce in the 1840. The Edinburgh & Northern Railway, a rival company whose main line ran from Burntisland to Newport-on-Tay near Dundee, constructed a competing branch line from Ladybank to Perth.

This really set the proverbial cat amongst the pigeons in rural Perthshire because, when the Perth & Crieff Direct Railway was proposed in 1845, the Edinburgh & Northern agreed to work this new line at a guaranteed dividend to shareholders of 4 per cent.

This was an example of a rival company to the Caledonian trying to expand into what the Caledonian regarded as its own rightful territory. The Caledonian responded fiercely and, as a result, the Perth & Crieff Direct Railway scheme was dropped.

In 1853 the Parliamentary Bill for the Crieff Junction Railway was passed. The line was planned to be opened in 1854, running from the Caledonian's main line at Crieff Junction to Crieff but it was not actually opened until 16th March, 1856. In the meantime, Muthill had no less than three station masters before the line even opened!

As a condition to letting the line pass through her estates, Lady Willoughby d'Eresby wished a private station to be built adjacent to Drummond Castle at which she could stop trains at her whim (in a similar fashion to what the Duke of Sutherland had already negotiated with the Highland Railway at his private station at Dunrobin). The Crieff Junction company objected to this and, as a result, it was forced to dig a deep well on its own property at Crieff in order to supply its locomotives with water necessary to make the return trip to the main line at Crieff Junction.

It also made sure that its line skirted Lady Willoughby d'Eresby's properties. This is the reason why Braco never got a station nearer than Greenloaning and why Muthill station was one and a half miles from the village!

Crieff Junction was renamed Gleneagles on 1st April, 1912. The station was rebuilt in its present form in 1919 but the famous railway-owned hotel nearby was not opened until 2nd June, 1924.

The Crieff Junction Railway was taken over by the Scottish Central Railway in 1865, shortly before the latter's amalgamation with the Caledonian in 1866.

Previous to the Crieff Junction Railway line being opened in 1856, a very considerable amount of traffic passed through Blairinroar from and to the South. Indeed, before the Scottish Central itself was opened in 1848, coals for Comrie had to be carried by road all the way from Bannockburn, a distance of 26 miles.

The Bill for another local railway, the Perth, Almond Valley & Methven Railway, had been authorised in 1856 and the line opened on 1st January, 1858. The line was absorbed by the Scottish North Eastern Railway in 1864 and operated by that company until its own absorption by the Caledonian in 1866.

There was a stagecoach link from Methven to Crieff until yet another railway company, the Crieff & Methven, opened its line from Crieff to Methven Junction on 21st May, 1866. This company too was taken over by the Caledonian Railway in 1869.

These takeovers were too late to prevent each of the companies building their own separate engine sheds adjacent to the old terminal station in Crieff.

The success of the Crieff Junction Railway in paying a dividend to shareholders of 5 per cent in the first half-year after its opening inspired local people to cast their eyes further west to open up the rich agricultural countryside between Crieff and Comrie. Their ultimate goal was Lochearnhead which was already connected by rail to the Callander & Oban line.

The first mention in the *Strathearn Herald* of a proposed railway to Comrie appeared as far back as 1st November, 1856 when it was reported that Messrs Stewart & Wood, in the service of Mr Brown, Civil Engineer of Perth, had completed a survey. This appears to have been the first of several surveys, all of which came to nothing.

On 22nd December, 1860 the *Strathearn Herald* again tried to stir up interest in the project in a leading article directed at the people of Comrie but to no avail.

Two years later, on 25th October, 1862, a public meeting was held in Comrie and was presided over by Mr Drummond of Drumearn. On this occasion much more interest was shown and it was resolved that:

> From previous surveys and calculations, it is certain that the line will be finished for £30,000 which shall be raised in £10 shares; and from the traffic there is every prospect of the line paying at least 5%.

Messrs Ironside & Graham, solicitors, Crieff, were appointed joint Secretaries and it was decided to go ahead with the project.

The meeting noted that Mr T.G. Stirling of Strowan, who was one of the most important landowners along the course of the line, was in favour of the proposed railway and would have moved the first resolution for its construction had he been able to be present that evening. At this time Thomas Graham Stirling was 51 years of age and had inherited the large estate of Strowan in 1837. His positive attitude towards the railway in 1862 contrasts significantly with his attitude nearly 30 years later when the proposals eventually came to fruition.

Fifteen days later it was reported in the *Strathearn Herald* that Mr Thomas Bouch and his assistants had nearly finished their survey but, owing to the lateness of the season, there would not be time to lodge a Bill in Parliament. It was now proposed to go for a direct line from Comrie to Methven to link up with the Perth, Almond Valley & Methven Railway which had reached the latter village on 1st January, 1858. However, when a separate railway was promoted between Crieff and Methven (the Crieff & Methven Junction Railway) by other parties and this was successful in obtaining an Act of Parliament for its construction, interest in the Comrie-Crieff railway project temporarily waned.

Thomas Bouch had at one time been Engineer and Manager of the Edinburgh & Northern Railway and, after this company expanded to become the Edinburgh, Perth and Dundee Railway, he had instituted the world's first public train ferries. These initially plied between Granton and Burntisland and subsequently between Tayport and Broughty Ferry as well. They provided an alternative and quicker route from Edinburgh to Dundee instead of going via Stirling and Perth, but the Victorian traveller of the 1850s needed a strong stomach to face the crossings of the Forth and Tay estuaries in wintertime!

In the 1850s Thomas Bouch had become an independent engineer and consultant and, as such, he had been engaged to construct the Crieff Junction Railway from the present-day Gleneagles station to Crieff. Despite a reputation for sloppiness in his work and lack of attention to detail which sometimes had embarrassing results when a line was inspected by a Board of Trade Inspector prior to opening, he was engaged by the Crieff and Comrie Railway Company to survey their line. He was always a bold engineer and his proposal was for a line of 5 miles, 7 furlongs and 8½ chains, (i.e. almost 6 miles) long which included a 300 yard-long tunnel through the high ground north-east of Thornhill.

Although nothing came of the scheme at that time, Thomas Bouch went from strength to strength in his engineering career until, in 1870, he was appointed designer of a railway bridge across the Tay from Wormit to Dundee. For a variety of reasons the bridge was not finished and opened for traffic until 1st June, 1878. In the meantime he was also appointed designer of a railway bridge across the Forth.

When completed, his Tay Bridge, which cost £350,000, was regarded as one of the engineering wonders of the world. At the end of June 1879 Queen Victoria travelled over the bridge and knighted its designer.

Sir Thomas's engineering career came to a spectacular and tragic end only six months later when, on 28th December in a gale unprecedented in local history, his bridge collapsed whilst a Sunday evening train was crossing with the loss of all its passengers and train crew - around 80 lives in all.

The subsequent Board of Trade inquiry unequivocally blamed Sir Thomas for the disaster. The inquiry panel comprised three members: two of them were engineers (Mr Barlow and Colonel Yolland of the Royal Engineers) but, because the bridge had fallen into the river, the third member was the Commissioner for Wrecks, Mr Rotheray.

Because the science of railway engineering was relatively new, the only independent people the Government could rely on who had experience of large-scale engineering work were military officers of the Corps of Royal Engineers. That is the reason why Royal Engineers officers carried out inquiries into railway accidents on behalf of the Board of Trade, a practice that survived until quite recent times.

Whilst the two professional engineers on the inquiry felt that Sir Thomas's design for the bridge was partly responsible for its collapse, they expressed reservations as to how much he himself should shoulder the blame for the poor workmanship of the contractors in actually building the bridge. Given the state of engineering technology in the 1870s, they, as engineers themselves, probably felt it was a case of 'Here, but for the grace of God, go I'.

Commissioner Rotheray was not so lenient. In his own separate report he stated that 'This bridge was badly designed, badly constructed and badly maintained, and that its downfall was due to inherent defects in the structure which must sooner or later have brought it down'. In his view, Sir Thomas Bouch was to blame on all counts.

This was the end of Thomas Bouch's professional career. Reviled in the popular press as a 'murderer in the gutters', his wife took him away to live in seclusion at Moffat where his health quickly deteriorated and he quietly died of a broken heart a few months later.

Needless to say, the work that had already begun on his design for a Forth Bridge was immediately stopped. A start had already been made by building a foundation on Inchgarvie Island; surmounted by a warning light the foundation stones stand to this day next to one of the piers of the present Forth Bridge.

In fairness to Bouch, a good number of his works stood the test of time. Probably the best of these were the magnificent wrought-iron viaducts he constructed over the Pennines at Belah and Deepdale on the line from Darlington to Tebay. This line was closed in the 1960s under the Beeching closures and the viaducts, then valuable for recycling as scrap material, had literally to be pulled down by huge machines.

To return to the Crieff and Comrie Railway, interest was revived in the following year (1863) when Colonel Williamson of Lawers became involved in the project for the first time. He issued a circular asking for subscriptions towards the undertaking and, within a month, the amount of £22,000 was reported to have been subscribed. At this point the estimated cost of the line was £32,000 and it was expected that the balance would be easily raised.

David Robertson Williamson was, at this time, 33 years old. He had inherited the Lawers estate in 1852 at the age of 22 from the widow of his great-uncle, Lord Balgray, who had been a judge of the Court of Session and who, in 1823, had rebuilt Lawers House in imitation of part of the Palace of Versailles. A year after succeeding to the estate he married the Honourable Selina Maria Morgan, second daughter of Sir Charles Morgan of Tredegar House, Newport, South Wales, who subsequently became the first Lord Tredegar. Selina's eldest brother, Godfrey, was soon to become famous for leading his regiment at the charge of the Light Brigade at Balaclava.

Along with the Dundas family, the Williamsons were one of the principal landowners in the Comrie area and the Colonel regarded it as his moral and social duty to do everything in his power to benefit the village.

His neighbouring landowner to the east was Sir Patrick Keith Murray of Ochtertyre and to the south was Thomas Graham Stirling of Strowan. He was particularly friendly with the latter's eldest son and heir, Tommy, and when the latter was killed at the battle of Tel-el-Kebir in 1882 whilst leading a charge of a section of the 'Black Watch' regiment, he immediately set out for southern Egypt to bring Tommy's body back from his grave on the battlefield so that it might lie with his ancestors in the family burial ground at Strowan. His mission was successful; Tommy's body was landed at Portsmouth and conveyed by special train to Crieff from where it was taken with a military escort to Strowan House.

An Act of Parliament for the new Crieff & Comrie Railway Company was obtained in 1865 and on 15th July the following paragraph appeared in the *Strathearn Herald*:

> It is said that the termini of the Crieff & Methven Junction Railway will embrace a general passenger station for all the railways into Crieff, namely the Crieff & Methven, Crieff Junction and Crieff & Comrie, and it is proposed to convert the present terminus of the Crieff Junction Railway into a general goods station. The Crieff & Comrie Railway Bill having the Royal assent, all the Companies will proceed immediately to make arrangements for the various stations.

The first Ordinary Meeting of the newly formed Crieff & Comrie Railway Company was held in the Queen's Hotel, Glasgow, at the end of December 1865. The business on this occasion was purely formal but at the end of January the following encouraging news was reported in the *Strathearn Herald*:

> Great exertions are being made by the promoters of this undertaking to get the line set agoing in March. The Directors and several others have doubled their original subscriptions and many shares have been taken in Comrie and neighbourhood in the last few days. Now is the time for those who wish to further the interest of the district to do so. It is to be regretted that some of the landowners in the district are doing very little if anything - the very men most interested.

Under the terms of the Act, the Scottish Central Railway, which was already working the Crieff & Methven Junction Railway, was authorised to subscribe for £20,000 of the stock and to work the line in perpetuity. It was to have its own representative on the Board of Directors. Unfortunately for this scheme, the Scottish Central Railway soon afterwards amalgamated with the much larger Caledonian Railway which was decidedly lukewarm towards the proposals.

Six months later it was reported that the Crieff & Comrie Railway's Directors had met in Glasgow with the Caledonian Railway's Directors to discuss preliminary arrangements for proceeding with the line. Their proposal was that the Caledonian should operate the line and provide locomotives and rolling stock in return for a percentage of the gross receipts.

The Crieff & Comrie's Directors had been particularly encouraged by a precognition made by William Veitch who was the Secretary of the Crieff Junction Railway Company. In it he said:

I have been Secretary of the Crieff Junction Railway Company for about nine years, and during that time I have resided in Crieff. I have also been Manager of the said Railway for about four years. The terminus of our Railway is at Crieff. It joins the Scottish Central Railway at Loaninghead, near Auchterarder, and thus connects Crieff with the Railway Systems of the Kingdom.

I know Comrie and the surrounding district well. The Village of Comrie is in a very thriving condition, and much frequented by summer visitors. The trade of the Town is considerable.

During last Summer and Autumn there were three Stage coaches running between Crieff and Comrie. Two of these ran twice a day each way, and the other one once. There is one Carrier daily who drives two carts. There is another with two carts twice a week, and another with two carts once a week. The two latter go to distances beyond Comrie. There are besides a great many private individuals who cart to Comrie on hire.

The country surrounding Comrie is very richly wooded, growing large quantities of excellent Standard Timber. A large traffic to the South in Timber has been carried on for sometime from the Comrie district. This has been more especially the case since the opening of the Crieff Junction Railway.

The country between Crieff and Comrie is rich in Agricultural resources, and might be much improved if proper facilities were afforded for the transmission of Lime, Coals, Tile, etc., etc.

The Comrie route is the outlet to the South for the extensive districts embracing Glenartney, Lochearnside and the Breadalbane country.

From my position I have favourable opportunities of judging of the resources of Comrie and that district as a traffic-producing country.

In 1864 the traffic over the Crieff Junction Railway, either coming from or going to the Comrie district was as follows, viz:- 15,000 Passengers, 2,500 tons General Merchandise, 2,200 tons Wood, 3,220 tons Minerals, besides Parcels, Horses, Carriages and Dogs, and Live Stock. Estimating these at the Revenue they would produce to the Crieff and Comrie Railway, you have as follows:-

	£	s.	d.
15,000 Passengers @ 9d.	562	10	0
2,500 tons General Merchandise @ 2s.	250	0	0
2,200 tons Wood @ 1s. 6d.	165	0	0
3,220 tons Minerals @ 1s. 3d.	201	5	0
Parcels, Horses, Carriages and Dogs, say	60	0	0
Live Stock, say	50	0	0
Annual Total	£1,288	15	0

If a Railway is made to Comrie this traffic will increase at least two-thirds in consequence of facilities and the reduction of present expenses	2,143	5	0
Local traffic between Comrie and Crieff and intermediate district which is not carried by the Crieff Junction Railway, say	1,500	0	0
	£3,643	5	0
Assuming that the working expenses of this traffic amount to 45 per cent	1,639	9	3
	£2,003	15	9

Which would apply a Dividend of 5 per cent, in the event of the Line being made, of £40,000.

So far as the public is concerned, besides the convenience and comfort of travelling and the rapid transport of Goods, etc., there will be a saving of 6*d.* on each Third-class Passenger, 3*s.* 6*d.* a ton on General Merchandise, 2*s.* 6*d.* a ton on Wood, 2*s.* 3*d.* a ton on Minerals, or in all of about £1,500 per annum on the existing traffic between the Crieff Junction Railway and Comrie and district, besides a great saving on the expense of existing local traffic.

A great many of the passengers who arrive at Crieff by the Crieff Junction Railway for Comrie and that district are obliged to hire at some of the Hotels.

Passengers have often complained to me about the want of Railway accommodation to Comrie.

There has been one Stage Coach twice a day to Comrie during Winter, and Passengers are often detained a long time waiting for the hour at which it leaves Crieff.

A great many of the tourists and people who come to the district for health have made enquiries at myself and our officials about Comrie, and a great proportion of them go to that district.

The construction of a Railway to Comrie would be a great public benefit and a great boon to the inhabitants of Comrie and that district, besides being a profitable undertaking for the Company.

On 3rd November, 1866, at the half-yearly meeting of the shareholders held in Crieff, it was stated that the Directors were prepared to take active measures for the construction of the line immediately after the ground had been cleared of the growing crops, so that by this time next year the railway would be nearly ready for opening. (Climatic conditions in the area must have been very unusual that year if there were still 'growing crops' in November!)

A fortnight later it was announced that active steps were now being taken to proceed with the formation of the line. The services of Mr Thomas Bouch, C.E., had been engaged and offers for contracts would shortly be advertised.

On 1st December the *Strathearn Herald* was reporting that all difficulties had been removed and that the hindrance lies now with the local officials. Subsequently it reported that:

On 22nd December the necessary papers were signed and the working plans are expected to be ready about the month of February or March. They conclude the report by stating: In regard to this subject, we are officially authorised to give an emphatic contradiction to the statement in a contemporary that there is not the least prospect when railway communication will be extended to Comrie.

The latest forecast was that navvies would start work in around two months' time.

The problems hinted at in the above paragraph and emphatically denied by the company finally came out into the open in the spring of the following year, 1867. On 20th April the *Strathearn Herald* reported that:

It appears that the construction of the Crieff & Comrie Railway has been abandoned in the meantime, and will not be proceeded with for some time to come. The Caledonian Railway are promoters of the undertaking to the extent of one half (£20,000) of the capital. It is said the delay has resulted from the small number of shares subscribed for in the district.

(The reference to the Caledonian being promoters of the undertaking arose from their inheritance of the Scottish Central's previously-given authorisation to subscribe for £20,000 stock in the proposed new company.) A nationwide depression had settled over new railway building and it was many years before public confidence was restored.

A half-yearly shareholders' meeting of the Crieff & Comrie Railway Company was held in Glasgow on 30th April, 1867 with Sir Patrick Keith Murray of Ochtertyre in the chair. He reported that their Engineer had nearly completed the plans and specifications of the works necessary for the construction of the line but, as the capital had not been fully subscribed, the Board had thought it expedient to obtain the sanction of the Caledonian to the works being proceeded with as it might be necessary to ask that company for additional funds to meet the expenses of the undertaking.

The Caledonian's reply was that, whilst they would like to see the line completed as soon as possible, railway affairs generally were depressed and they could not undertake to supply the balance of the capital. They therefore recommended that the project be put in abeyance.

The Crieff & Comrie Directors reluctantly decided that they could not go ahead with the line in spite of well over half of the capital having been subscribed. So ended five years' work on the project, the nearest that Comrie had so far come to having a rail connection with the outside world.

Over the next few years several more attempts were made to revive the project. In 1877 another public meeting was held and a committee was appointed which reported in April the following year that all the local landed proprietors were in favour, but the Directors of the Caledonian Railway would not in the meantime give any support to the movement.

In October 1880 Colonel Williamson made another effort to promote a line between Crieff and Comrie. His circular to prospective shareholders is worth quoting at some length because it sets out the economic reasons for building the line.

It is believed that the time has now arrived when the project may be revived with success. The reasons which led to the movement of 1864-7 still exist, and have acquired much greater force from the largely-increased population and traffic along the proposed route, while it is believed that the difficulties which were experienced at that time are not likely to be felt now, as it is understood that the Caledonian Railway Company is at present in a position that they can materially forward the scheme.

The proposed line will pass along one of the most popular Tourist Routes in Scotland. Leaving the town of Crieff, the Capital of Strathearn, the Railway will pass through the picturesque lands of Strowan, also Ochtertyre, the seat of Sir Patrick Keith Murray, Bart., and rendered classic by the poetic genius of Burns. The line will afterwards pass Clathick, the seat of Captain Colquhoun; and Lawers, the seat of Colonel David R. Williamson, both of which places vie with Ochtertyre in the magnificence of their Highland and Lowland scenery. The Village of Comrie possesses very great attractions to Tourists, and has extensive hotel and villa accommodation, which can easily be extended to meet the increased demand which would undoubtedly follow the railway communication with the south.

The Terminus of the proposed new Railway would be within four miles of St. Fillans, at the foot of Loch Earn; and the rapid extension of this picturesque Village within the past few years justifies the hope that the Railway may, at no distant date, be profitably extended to this favourite summer resort. Connection with the Callander & Oban Railway can be maintained by Coach, - or, if desirable, Steamer on Loch Earn, - there being a Station on this line at the head of the Loch.

The traffic to be carried on by the Crieff and Comrie Railway would consist of:

First - Tourists from Glasgow, Edinburgh, Dundee, and from England, travelling via Perth and Crieff Junction to Oban and intermediate stations, and vice versa. The tourist season extends from June to October, during which months large numbers of tourists pass over the proposed route by public Coaches and hired conveyances, on their way to Oban, - or on a Circular Tour via Perth, Crieff, Comrie, St. Fillans, Lochearnhead and Callander - a tour which is every year becoming more popular, and which has been opened up since the proposed New Railway between Crieff and Comrie was before the public. The scenery along the route of the proposed New Railway is of the most enchanting description. From the fertile valley of the Earn rise numberless rugged hills and gigantic mountains; and new beauties in loch, river, mountain, glen and valley open up at every turn. Within the past few years the route has become so popular with tourists that the Caledonian Railway Company run a number of Coaches throughout the season between Crieff, through Comrie, and the station on the Callander and Oban line at Lochearnhead. These are largely taken advantage of, notwithstanding an increase in the fares since the route was opened. The fares are necessarily high on account of the expense of Coaching so many miles of the journey; and it is unquestionable that, with the increased facilities and the cheaper fares which would follow the opening of this line, the tourist traffic would be developed to a very much larger extent.

Second - In addition to this large tourist traffic, there is a considerable regular passenger traffic between Crieff and Comrie, and the extensive districts which surround these places. This traffic is at present carried on by public Coach and hired conveyances, while a very great number are compelled to perform the journey on foot. There is also an extensive and increasing traffic in goods, which is conducted by public carriers and private conveyances. It is believed that the diversion of this traffic alone would yield a handsome income, while experience proves that the increased facilities and cheaper rates which the railways afford create a vast amount of traffic that did not previously exist.

Third - The districts between Crieff and Comrie, and for many miles beyond the terminus of the proposed Railway, is rich in agricultural produce, and an immense number of Sheep and Cattle, and vast quantities of Timber are constantly being forwarded to the southern markets. At present the markets can only be reached by long and fatiguing journeys by road, - a circumstance which greatly hinders the development of the capabilities of the districts, by limiting the facilities and increasing the expense of reaching the markets.

Fourth - Large quantities of Wool are sent to the southern markets from the districts to be traversed by the proposed new line, and considerable quantities of Oilcake, Agricultural Manures, Coals and General Goods are imported into the district.

The route of the proposed new line was surveyed when the Act of 1865 was obtained. It was then found that no part of the proposed line presented any engineering difficulties.

It is proposed to form a Company with a capital of £30,000, and it has been suggested that the number of Shares into which the Capital should be divided shall be 3,000, the amount of each share being £10.

It is expected that the proposed line will pay a dividend of Five or Six per cent.

A form asking the recipients to state how many Shares they would provisionally agree to purchase accompanied the circular. Unfortunately, several landed proprietors objected to the proposed line and, once again, nothing came of the project.

Above: Colonel D.R. Williamson, Chairman of the
Crieff & Comrie Railway Company.

Right: Thomas Graham Stirling of Strowan (1811-
1896). He fought against the building of the Crieff &
Comrie Railway unless the promoters built him a
new road bridge that would take unwanted road
traffic away from the vicinity of his mansion. He lost!

Author

Negotiations with local landowners continued over the years. One of the most difficult to deal with was Thomas Graham Stirling of Strowan, which was all the more surprising in view of his close personal friendship with Colonel Williamson. Nevertheless, he made several stipulations if the railway was to cross what was only a small portion of his property. In February 1888 he stated that:

I agree to the railway scheme on the following conditions - that no station be placed on the Trowan side of the Monument Hill, that the line should be carried through the hollow on the north east of the Monument Hill, that a station be placed somewhere at Thornhill, that the line should be kept as near the river embankment as possible without going out of the straight from one angle to the other outside the old water course, that I am held free from incurring any responsibility as to the upholding of the river embankment.

Yet another Public Meeting was held in January 1888, this time in the Mission Room at Comrie, when the following named gentlemen were present:

Captain Dundas of Dalchonzie
Revd Macpherson (Established Church)
Carolus Home Graham Stirling of Strowan
Robert MacNaughtan of Cowden
Peter Drummond of Drumearn
Peter Brough, Dundas House
Dr Temple, Comrie
Messrs Davie, St Fillans
Mr Kemp, Easter Dalginross
Mr McIntyre, Muirend
Mr Boston, Balmuick
Mr Campbell, Tullybannocher
Mr Phillips, Dalchonzie
Mr McIntyre, Cuilt
Mr McIntyre, merchant

Mr C. McLaren, slater
Mr C. Robertson, merchant
Mr J. Crerar, merchant
Mr J. Graham, merchant
Mr J. Comrie, joiner
Mr J. McIntyre, butcher
Mr W. Drummond, shoemaker
Mr J. Comrie, merchant
Mr A. Gray, baker
Mr J.W. Drummond, joiner
Mr W. Gibson, teacher
Mr D. Hamilton, Royal Hotel
Mr J. McNeil, Commercial Hotel
Mr P. Sharp, builder

Apologies for absence were received from Colonel Williamson of Lawers, Colonel Colquhoun of Clathick, Mr D.K. Murray of Westerton, Ochtertyre, and Mr Sandison of St Fillans.

Colonel Williamson, in his letter of regret, avowed that he was as interested as ever in the railway and would personally subscribe for three or four thousand pounds-worth of shares in a new company. The other absentees, whilst not going so far as the Colonel in terms of financial commitments, nevertheless gave their wholehearted support to the project.

Captain Dundas took the chair and the meeting began by discussing the likelihood of the Caledonian Railway Company agreeing to build a branch line from Crieff to Comrie on the lines of proposals previously put to them, namely that the landowners along the line of the proposed railway would give or sell their lands cheaply.

However, unlike earlier discussions with the Scottish Central Railway and their successors, the Caledonian, the promoters now had another card in their hand. This was the arrival in Perth of the North British Railway, the

Caledonian's bitter commercial rival, which was on the lookout for opportunities to expand into the Caledonian's heartland.

It was proposed at the meeting that, should the Caledonian not be willing to build and work the proposed extension to Comrie, the North British should be invited to build and work the line.

This was a blatant attempt to blackmail the Caledonian! The North British was already preparing plans for what is now the West Highland Railway, from Craigendoran up to Crianlarich and on to Fort William. In railway strategic terms, it would have made political sense for it to build a line westwards from Perth to meet up with its new railway. This would have cut across the heart of what the Caledonian regarded as its own territory.

The meeting discussed at great length the pros and cons of whether the line they were asking the Caledonian to build should terminate at Comrie or should be carried on to St Fillans or Lochearnhead. The members in favour of terminating the line at Comrie said that if the line was carried further westwards, passengers would be tempted to travel through the region and so Comrie's hotels and businesses would gain no benefit whatsoever from the railway. On the other hand, there was a feeling that the Caledonian would not be prepared to put any money into the project unless it linked up with the Callander & Oban line (which it already controlled) in the region of Lochearnhead.

The meeting decided that a deputation comprising Captain Dundas, Mr Carolus Graham Stirling, Mr MacNaughtan, Mr Davie and Mr Macpherson, should approach Mr Bolton, the Chairman of the Caledonian Railway, to ascertain how much they might be prepared to subscribe towards the construction of the proposed line.

Mr Carolus Graham Stirling objected to his inclusion in the deputation on the grounds that he was simply representing his father at the meeting and his father was opposed to the railway. The other members countered by saying that he was therefore an ideal person to have on the sub-committee so that he could express his father's views!

It was also agreed that if no satisfactory reply were received from the Caledonian, the sub-committee would have the power to approach the North British with the same proposals.

The deputation duly travelled to Glasgow for a meeting with the Caledonian's Chairman, Mr Bolton, armed with letters from local landowners promising that they would sell their land at a reasonable cost.

Mr Bolton received them politely but was unimpressed with their arguments; he wanted them to bring a large sum of money with them before he would consider committing the Caledonian to building the railway. He told them to go back home and find out how much money they could raise locally. When they could tell him that, his company would take a look at the proposed line and work out how much it would cost to build. When the visitors hinted that his rivals, the North British Railway, might be interested in the scheme, he told the deputation that they were welcome to try them!

The deputation returned home and called another public meeting at which they reported gloomily on their lack of success.

After lengthy debate it was decided that the a letter should be sent to Mr Bolton, asking whether the Caledonian would be prepared to subscribe £20,000 or £25,000 to assist in the construction of a railway from Crieff to Comrie if the public raised a further £10,000 and the landowners sold their land on terms similar to those they had agreed when Colonel Williamson had approached them in 1880, namely agricultural land at 30 years purchase and feued* land at 22 years purchase.

The Chairman of the meeting, Captain Dundas, wrote the letter but the Caledonian's reply was not exactly encouraging. He received the following letter dated 7th March, 1888 from the Secretary's office:

> Sir – Your letter of 22nd February and its accompanying 'extract minute of public meeting in connection with the proposed railway from Crieff to Comrie of 20th ult.' were yesterday considered by my Board, and I am desired to say that they are not prepared at present to come under the engagement proposed by the minute; but if the gentlemen resident in the district make the line at their own cost, this Company will, if required, be ready to work it.

The letter was signed by the Secretary, Archibald Gibson.

The *Strathearn Herald* reported that after expressing disappointment at the reply, the meeting agreed to approach the North British Railway Company (the Caledonian's biggest rival) and ascertain if they would be willing to give assistance to the project. No details remain regarding this approach but it cannot have been fruitful because nothing further was heard of it.

The public coach timetable in that year was as follows:

Comrie	dep.	8.50 am (6.15 am on Mondays) and 3.30 pm
Crieff	dep.	10.20 am and 6.00 pm

The journey time was about one hour.

The Caledonian Railway's coach times were:

Crieff Station	*dep.*	10.25 am	Lochearnhead Station	*arr.*	2.55 pm
Lochearnhead Station	*dep.*	11.40 am	Crieff Station	*arr.*	4.25 pm

Over an hour's break was allowed at St Fillans in both directions.

The proposal that eventually brought the railway to Comrie was initiated by Colonel Williamson in 1889.

The *Strathearn Herald*, ever hopeful, wrote under the heading of 'The Proposed Crieff & Comrie Railway' that:

> The good people of Comrie who in the year 1856 rejoiced over the first proposal of railway extension to their village, having grown grey since that time and hope deferred, might well have made the heart sick of the whole affair; yet it must be confessed that they have manfully persevered amidst many failures during the last 33 years to attain their objective.

Rail passengers in Crieff were all in favour of the new railway because it meant that their existing terminal station, which fronted onto King Street,

---

* Land leased on a perpetual lease at a fixed rent.

would have to be rebuilt as a 'through' station. Complaints about the inadequacy of the present station were legion as, for example, this report in the *Strathearn Herald* on 3rd August, 1889:

> This week the traffic at the railway station, owing to the large number of passengers going and coming, has been very heavy and trains very late. The wretched station, and especially the platform accommodation, is causing much inconvenience to passengers, it being almost impossible to move about owing to the confusion of carriages, luggage, etc.

This was followed a fortnight later with a reference to:

> That collection of wooden huts called the Crieff Railway Station which, for more than a quarter of a century, has been an eyesore to everyone and its surroundings a danger to not a few.

So far as Comrie's attitude to the railway was concerned, it must be admitted that until now their citizens had shown a marked reluctance to match their enthusiasm for a railway with subscribing for it in hard cash. In this new initiative the district was well canvassed from the outset and the shares were priced at a sum that most working men could afford. Colonel Williamson himself subscribed for 5,000 shares, G.C. Gilchrist of Aberuchill subscribed for 1,000 shares and both R. McNaughtan of Cowden and Peter Drummond of Drumearn subscribed for 500 shares.

In May 1889 the Directors of the Caledonian Railway Company agreed to work the new railway if ever it was built but they still refused to offer any financial assistance whatsoever towards the funding of the line. In July they refused to meet a deputation of the promoters who wished to discuss with them, prior to issuing their Prospectus, the best way that the Caledonian could support them. The Caledonian Directors replied that their railway could not subscribe and therefore a meeting to consider the point would be useless.

The local promoters realised that they had to 'go it alone'. They issued a new Prospectus and lodged a Parliamentary Bill in November 1889.

The earlier Prospectus of the Crieff & Comrie Railway Company had shown an authorised share capital of £40,000 in 40,000 shares of £1 each, comprised of 21,000 Ordinary Shares at par and 15,000 4 per cent Preference Shares at £1 1s. each. However, the new Prospectus proposed an authorised share capital of £45,000 and power to borrow another £15,000.

The abridged Prospectus read as follows:

Provisional Directors:
Colonel D R Williamson of Lawers, JP and DL Perthshire (Chairman)
Sir Robert D. Moncrieffe, Bart, of Moncrieffe, JP and DL Perthshire
Colonel Drummond Moray of Blair Drummond, JP, ex MP of Perthshire
Robert MacNaughtan Esq. of Cowden, JP
William R. MacGregor Esq, Provost of Crieff, JP
James Crerar Esq., Comrie
Peter Brough Esq., Dundas House, Comrie
Peter Comrie Esq., Comrie
William MacIntyre Esq., Comrie

Engineer: John Young CE, Perth
Bankers: Town & County Bank Ltd.
Solicitors: R. & J. Robertson & Dempster, Perth
Auditors: Thomson, Jackson, Gourlay & Taylor, CA, Glasgow
Secretary: D.N. Shaw, 16 High Street, Perth

Engineer's estimate:	Construction	£26,883
	Land and Houses	4,460
	Parliamentary, etc. exps.	3,000
		34,343
	Contingency	3,130
		£37,473

The Directors proposed to raise the money, plus £900 further provision, as described above. The minimum subscription would be 10 x £1 Shares.

Estimated Revenue:	Passengers and Mails	£1,600
	Parcels, carriages, horses and dogs	250
	Livestock	350
	Goods and Minerals	1,400
		£3,600

[This equated to £11 16s. revenue per mile per week, considerably less than most established railways were achieving.]

Working Expenses @ 50 per cent of revenue	1,800
Interest on estimated total expenditure @ say 4 per cent	1,500
	£3,300

Giving an estimated surplus of	£300

A Public Meeting was held in Comrie to promote the undertaking to the general public. Press comment was generally very favourable and the *Strathearn Herald* commented on 18th May that:

The promoters of this latest attempt to obtain a railway to Comrie have wisely started it on a very popular basis, by making the shares so reasonable an amount that almost every working man can embark in the scheme, and we have no doubt that if it can be as economically carried out as proposed in the prospectus, the shareholders will get all that is proposed them as a return for their money. We do not at present go into figures, but it may be interesting to intending shareholders to know that one landed proprietor on the line of railway is to give his ground free, and most, if not all, the others are agreeable to give theirs at very reasonable rates. It may also be important to state that several gentlemen have signified their intention of becoming large shareholders to the amount, we understand, of about an eighth of the whole capital required. Comrie has been too long isolated from railway communication, and from its growing importance as a summer resort, and situated as it is amongst some of the finest Scottish scenery, it would undoubtedly attract more traffic, and become in consequence an additional feeder to the Caledonian Railway system. Of course, to make it perfect in this respect, the line would require to be carried all the way to Lochearnhead, and this, we doubt not, will be done ere long. In the meantime, money is required to make it a success, and at the price the shares are offered, the people of Comrie and surrounding district ought at once to show an example in this respect and their confidence in the scheme by going in largely for the stock. If they do so, the outside public will not be slow to follow so good an example by those who know the capabilities of the district.

The *Crieff Journal* was similarly encouraging on 21st June:

The village of Comrie, situated in the centre of one of the loveliest districts in the country, has for many years been handicapped in the race with other towns similarly favoured by nature for desirability as a place of residence, but more particularly for popularity as a summer resort, on account of its having no railway communication with our large centres of industry. If the Crieff and Comrie Railway be formed, as there is every prospect of it being, it will undoubtedly confer an incalculable boon on the district. The delightful situation of the village would draw many to take up their residence in it. In Dalginross there is a large number of most desirable feus, which would have been taken up long ere now but for the want of railway communication. Then, as regards summer visitors, it would be impossible to calculate the number of people resident in our large towns who would be attracted by the natural beauties of Comrie were they in direct communication with it. The tourist traffic, too, would be immensely increased. In short, the connecting of Crieff and Comrie by railway would be the beginning of a grand era of prosperity in the latter's history. We, therefore, hail with unmixed satisfaction the proposal to extend the railway to Comrie, certain that it will prove more beneficial to the district, and confident that it will meet with marked success.

However, the *Perth Advertiser* was not so enthusiastic. On 22nd May, 1889 it wrote:

On paper this is a very satisfactory balance sheet; whether it will be realised in the event of the construction of the line is quite another matter. If it should the new railway will be quite unique in its earnings. A revenue of £1,500 from passengers means a traffic of this kind of a most abnormally thriving kind – something like the conveyance of forty or fifty thousand passengers. How £1,500 is to be raised from the conveyance of goods and minerals is another mystery. The Callander & Oban Railway, which is twelve times the length of the proposed new line, passes through a district not unlike that of Crieff, and possesses the decided advantage of being a through line, only earns something like £100 per mile in this kind of traffic. Yet the new Crieff line is expected to earn two and a half times as much, or £250 per mile. The total earnings of the Callander & Oban line amount to something like £320 per mile; but the Crieff line is expected to earn for all kinds of traffic about £600 per mile. We do not believe that it will; and we think that the promoters would have been nearer the mark had they put down the expected earnings of the proposed line at £2,000, or £2,500 at the very outside. This balance would give a dividend of 2% upon the share capital, and if the shareholders get this, which is extremely doubtful, they would be very lucky.

The promoters vigorously set about canvassing support amongst influential figures. They had a fair amount of success, receiving many letters of support accompanied by applications for shares, such as the following letter from a subscriber in Grangemouth:

I wish every success to your efforts in getting this much-needed, and long spoken of, railway made to Comrie.
I think that in this lies the only hope of improving Comrie and its neighbourhood.
You will please enter me for fifty shares.

Not everyone responded in a positive vein. In a letter dated 18th July, Colonel Williamson received short shrift from Sir Donald Currie, the MP for West Perthshire:

I daresay you will see a copy of the letter which Mr D.N. Shaw has written to me under date the 14th instant to which I have sent an answer today.

In your last letter you spoke about a large number who would, with yourself, give me political support, but this consideration should not weigh in the question whether with every desire to assist the good people of Crieff and Comrie I should make an investment and lead other people to invest in what as a short line I am informed cannot be made to pay.

Sir Donald had been 'pencilled in' for 350 shares but did not subscribe.

A similar response was received from James Thompson, General Manager of the Caledonian Railway Company:

I have your letter of the 29th instant and in reply beg to say that I shall be very glad to arrange to see you if so desired about the working agreement, but I gather from your letter that you wish to discuss the question of the Caledonian Company subscribing to the capital of the Crieff & Comrie Company.

As this is rather a matter for the Directors to deal with, and while it would be a pleasure for me to meet you, I fear that I could not at the present time recommend my Directors to subscribe to the Crieff & Comrie undertaking.

Some were supportive but unable to help, as in the reply from Thomas Watters who was a farmer at Glenample:

The proposed railway will be a great boon to me and I trust it will soon be made, but my balances - like most farmers here - have unfortunately been on the wrong side for several years and I cannot afford to invest any money.

Eventually he did subscribe for 10 shares.

By 1890 the project had gained enough support for its promoters to submit a Parliamentary Bill for the formation of a new Crieff & Comrie Railway Company. Objections were received from Thomas Graham Stirling of Strowan, the Perthshire County Road Trustees and the East Coast railway companies so, as a contended Bill, it had to be examined by a committee of MPs.

A view of Comrie from the south in the late 19th century.   *Author's Collection*

The Crieff & Comrie Railway Company.

Incorporated by Special Act of Parliament, 53 and 54 Vict., cap. 122, Session 1890: Whereby the liability of the Shareholders is limited to the amount of their Shares, and incorporating the Companies Clauses Consolidation (Scotland) Act, 1845, and other Acts.

Authorised Share Capital,—£45,000,

Divided into **9,000** Shares of £5 each, with Borrowing Powers to the extent of £15,000.

£40,000

OF THE SHARE CAPITAL HAVE ALREADY BEEN SUBSCRIBED.

ISSUE OF BALANCE OF SHARE CAPITAL AT PAR.

Payable **12s 6d** per Share on Application ; **12s 6d** per Share on Allotment,

And the balance by Calls not exceeding £1 per Share at intervals of not less than Two Calendar Months, with option of payment in full on Allotment.

DIRECTORS.

COLONEL D. R. WILLIAMSON OF LAWERS, J.P. AND D.L., PERTHSHIRE, *Chairman.*
SIR ROBT. D. MONCREIFFE, BART. OF MONCREIFFE, J.P. AND D.L., PERTHSHIRE.
COLONEL HOME DRUMMOND OF BLAIR DRUMMOND, J.P. AND EX-M.P., PERTHSHIRE.
ROBERT M'NAUGHTAN, ESQ. OF COWDEN, J.P., PERTHSHIRE.
JAMES CRERAR, ESQ., MERCHANT, COMRIE, PERTHSHIRE.
PETER BROUGH, ESQ., C.C., DUNDAS HOUSE, COMRIE, PERTHSHIRE.

ENGINEER.
JOHN YOUNG, M.INST. C.E., PERTH.

BANKERS.
THE CLYDESDALE BANK, LTD., GLASGOW, and Branches.

SOLICITORS.
R. & J. ROBERTSON & DEMPSTER, TOWN AND COUNTY BANK BUILDINGS, PERTH.

AUDITORS.
THOMSON, JACKSON, GOURLAY, & TAYLOR, C.A., GLASGOW.
ROBERT MORISON, ACCOUNTANT, PERTH.

SECRETARY.
D. N. SHAW, F.I.S., 98 BATH STREET, GLASGOW.

OFFICES.
98 BATH STREET, GLASGOW.

Cover page of the Crieff & Comrie Railway Prospectus, 1890.

Chapter Three

The Crieff and Comrie Railway Bill, 1890

When the Crieff & Comrie Railway Bill reached Parliament it was examined by a Select Committee of MPs under the chairmanship of Sir Julian Goldsmid, Bart. The other members of the committee were Mr Shepherd Cross, Mr Ballantyne and Mr Leveson Gower.

The objections of the Great Northern and North Eastern railway companies were soon dealt with. They were only concerned with establishing running powers over the proposed line and, at the time, they appeared satisfied with the assurances they were given.

The Perthshire Road Trustees were concerned about the possible effect of increased traffic over the old road bridge at Strowan for which they were responsible. This was linked to Mr Graham Stirling's claim and the two were dealt with together.

The background to the 80-year-old Laird of Strowan's objections was twofold.

Firstly, he did not wish to see any part of the railway from his mansion house at Strowan. It would seem that he had supported the earlier plans of 1862 because the line involved building a 300 yds-long tunnel through Monument Hill that would have kept trains out of sight from his house. Now the revised line, on which the length of the tunnel was reduced to 90 yards, would have brought them within his view, albeit for less than a minute, and he strongly objected to this intrusion.

Secondly and more importantly, the public road passed immediately in front of Strowan House and crossed the Earn by a picturesque old bridge a few yards away to the north. Until recently the old market cross had been situated nearby but he had managed to have the market transferred to Crieff. Now he wished to have the public road diverted to a new location out of sight of his mansion and he saw the coming of the railway as a golden opportunity to have this done at no expense to himself. He reasoned that if he insisted on a station or freight siding being built at nearby Thornhill as a condition of allowing the railway to cross his land, the extra traffic this would generate would be too much for the old bridge to carry. He drew up a map showing his proposal for diverting the road and building a new bridge across the Earn further downstream and submitted this to the committee in support of his objections.

The evidence laid before the committee by both parties is quoted here at some length because it gives a contemporary picture of conditions in the area at that time, albeit somewhat coloured by each side's claims! Mr Graham Stirling's case rested solely on his claim that the bridge was insufficiently strong to take the increased traffic and therefore it was the railway company's responsibility to replace it, whereas the railway company retorted that the bridge had proved itself strong enough for normal traffic and it was the road commissioners' responsibility to make any improvements.

The road commissioners, for their part, came under fire from both sides for having neglected maintenance of the bridge for many years past!

Comrie village centre in the 1860s, 30 years before the arrival of the railway. Note the observatory on the roof of Brough & Macpherson's shop.   *Author's Collection*

The old Strowan bridge *c.*1900. The dark marks on the side of the bridge are the iron clamps inserted to hold the bridge together.   *Author's Collection*

STROWAN BRIDGE, CRIEFF.

Parliamentary proceedings started on 24th April, 1890 with a speech by Mr Pember on behalf of the promoters. He described Comrie as,

. . . having become a very favourite place of summer resort . . . a very large number of persons visit Comrie every year, a great number of thousands, I think it is about from 15,000 to 20,000. Building is largely going on, and besides the number of visitors who visit or live at Comrie itself, there are a number of glens which converge upon Comrie in which there are farms. For both of them and for the important visiting population I have mentioned, all the supplies have now to be carted from Crieff, at considerable expense. Generally I may describe it as a place of growing importance, to which it is only a matter of remark and wonder that no railways have been made there long ago.

Mr Pember went on to say:

. . . with respect to these farms which I have mentioned, we expect to derive from them a considerable amount of traffic; there are very large sheep runs, and a great quantity of sheep are sent to Perth and to the southern markets, and also it is known to be a great place for timber; for which again there is a considerable demand in the southern markets, and also there is a considerable amount of wool grown. We expect a return traffic in agricultural matters such as feeding stuffs, artificial manure and so on. In short, there is very little doubt that what with passengers and these various items, a very good revenue will be derived from them.

Mr Graham Stirling's petition stated that he,

. . . is proprietor of the estate of Strowan . . . and the said proposed railway is intended to pass for upwards of two miles through the said estate, and within a short distance of the mansion house thereon where your Petitioner resides. The said proposed railway, insofar as it passes through your Petitioner's estate, has been laid out in a most injurious and objectionable manner, and so as seriously to interfere with the enjoyment and use thereof for residential and agricultural purposes. The amenity of the mansion house, which has of late years been enlarged and improved at great expense, would be seriously diminished, if not destroyed.

Mr Pember then turned to the question of the Strowan bridge whose strength was also the subject of the petition from the Road Trustees. Their petition read:

The said bridge is the only bridge over the River Earn, between Crieff and Comrie, on both sides of the River Earn, and this bridge is the connecting link between them. The said bridge is an old bridge of three arches, between 50 and 60 yards in length, and is known as the Strowan Bridge. It is a most important connection between the two sides of the river and any interference therewith, or proposals to stop up the same, would be injurious to the district and inconvenient to the inhabitants . . . In the event of the Promoters of the Bill not diverting the said road and substituting the road shown on the deposited plans . . . the Strowan Bridge would not be sufficient to carry the traffic to and from a station at or near the said point . . .

Mr Pember told the committee that the real interpretation of the Road Trustees' petition was that the Trustees knew that the bridge was in a tumbledown condition and that they had not done their duty in the past to maintain it properly. It was shored up in all sorts of ways to keep it on its legs and some day or other there would be a catastrophe. He had been told that, not

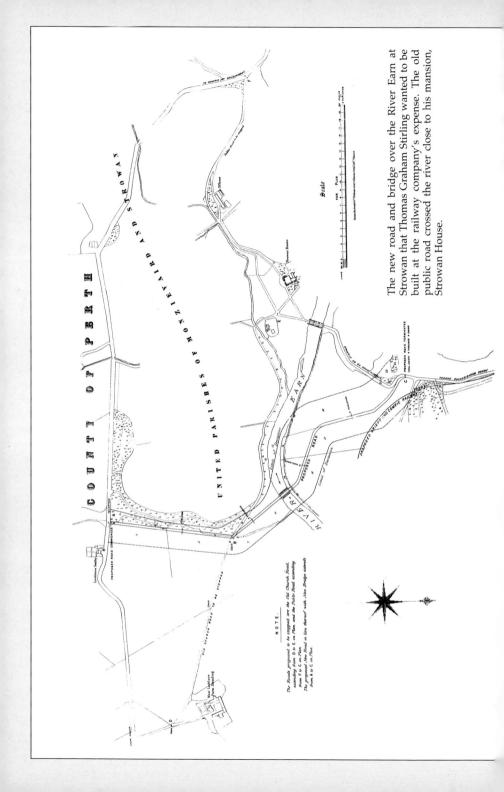

The new road and bridge over the River Earn at Strowan that Thomas Graham Stirling wanted to be built at the railway company's expense. The old public road crossed the river close to his mansion, Strowan House.

long ago, a carter had wanted to take a cart laden merely with oats across the bridge and had been warned by an officer of the Trustees not to risk it!

The question really boiled down to what could be defined as ordinary traffic. The railway promoters contended that the bridge was unfit for ordinary traffic, which would include increased traffic resulting from the railway's coming and so the bridge should be rebuilt or strengthened at the Trustees' expense, whilst the latter contended that the railway would bring exceptionally heavy loads for which the promoters should provide a new bridge at their own expense.

It was not as if the promoters *wanted* a station or a siding at Thornhill!

They didn't! They knew it would be unprofitable and the only reason why Thomas Graham Stirling was trying to insist on one was to try to get his road diversion and new bridge approved by Parliament at the railway promoters' expense.

On the following morning Colonel Williamson took the stand. He described himself as a Justice of the Peace for Perthshire and the owner of around 35,000 acres of land in the Comrie area.

Describing Comrie, he said there were three very good hotels and two others. Two of the hotels had been built within the past five years. A great number of new houses had been built by those interested in the village and by those doing business in the village, most of them as personal residences rather than as houses to let to summer visitors. The public road was continuously thronged with visitors, the hotels were usually full and it was difficult even now (in April) to find a house still to let for the summer. Visitors came from as far afield as Devonshire to enjoy the relaxation and the scenery.

When asked what facilities existed for these visitors to reach Comrie he replied that there were two public coaches but an immense number of private carriages had to be hired by visitors to bring them from the railway terminus at Crieff into the village. The public coaches made three regular journeys every day and as many as six at busy times but there were just too many visitors for them to carry. If the visitors, especially the poorer ones, could not board a coach or afford to hire a carriage, they had to walk the seven miles to Comrie. As regards education, there was only a primary school in the village so parents wishing their older children to have a higher standard of education had to board them with families in Crieff.

He went on to say that, apart from the present export of potatoes, wool, sheep and livestock, considerable amounts of timber, lime, slate and other building materials were available in the area for exporting to other parts of Britain if only they had railway facilities, whilst the price of coal brought to the village could be cut from 4s. 6d. per ton to around 9d.

As for Mr Graham Stirling's objection to seing the train from his windows, the Colonel pointed out that he would only see it in winter, end-on at a distance of around 500 yards from his house, whilst in summer the foliage would screen it completely.

The discussion now moved onto the question of the proposed diversion of the road away from Strowan House and the building of a new bridge at the railway company's expense.

Colonel Williamson's answers to his questioners were a masterpiece of obfuscation, being a mixture of feigned innocence, stonewalling and aggression. They are an absolute delight to read in the Parliamentary papers.

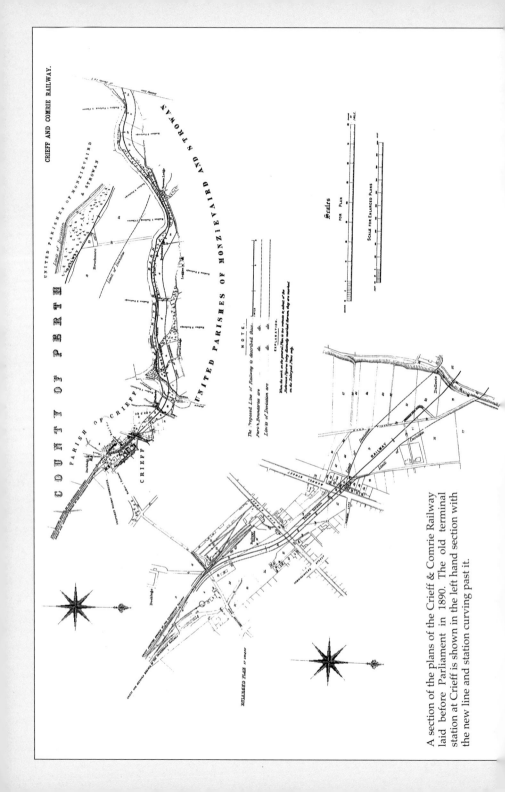

A section of the plans of the Crieff & Comrie Railway laid before Parliament in 1890. The old terminal station at Crieff is shown in the left hand section with the new line and station curving past it.

He began by agreeing that the bridge was incapable of bearing the heavy traffic that would result from a station at Thornhill. He then went on to ask what was the station they were talking about, because the railway company did not wish to build a station, or even a siding, at that location.

He finished by accusing the Road Trustees of attempting to pick the pockets of a small railway undertaking by trying to get them to replace, at a cost of around £5,000, a bridge that they themselves had neglected their duty to maintain as well as a new road. When asked whether he was prepared to agree that the bridge as it presently stood was equal to the light traffic that currently went over it, his reply was robust:

> No, I do not think it is. I believe it ought to have been pitched down the river years ago, and if we had had a proper engineer, depend upon it, it would have been done years ago! He has patched it and patched it up simply because the bridge is ornamental and rustic and pretty to look at!

The opposition then questioned the Colonel's experience of engineering but he soon silenced them with a list of his engineering experience over the past 50 years! When asked why he had not brought the matter of the bridge to the trustees' attention many years earlier, he charmed his questioners by referring to his long-standing personal friendship with Thomas Graham Stirling and said that he had not wished to upset him.

After concluding their questioning of Colonel Williamson and a number of other witnesses who accompanied him to London and who all corroborated his answers, it was the turn of the railway company's Engineer, Mr John Young, to be questioned. After a number of questions concerning his layout of the line and modifications he had already agreed at Mr Graham Stirling's request, the questioning moved to the condition of the Strowan bridge.

In answer to a question about the condition of the bridge, Mr Young said that it was in a very rickety condition and should not be there; it should have been renewed long ago. When asked if it would be safe for a brake loaded with tourists to cross it, he replied that he would not care to be one of its passengers!

The Chairman commented facetiously that if this caused the bridge to collapse, at least it would economise on the cost of pulling it down!

Mr Young went on to explain that a number of stones had already fallen from the arches of the bridge and more looked as if they were about to fall. The bridge was clamped together with iron.

The final witness was George Miller Cunningham, an eminent civil engineer with wide experience of bridges, who appeared in support of the promoters. In his opinion the bridge was quite unfit for heavy traffic as, in his words, 'It is patched up altogether, one stone clamped to another'. He asserted that anyone who had ever been under the bridge and seen its parlous state would never drive over the top!

The local surveyor of roads was the next to be questioned. He stated that the bridge had originally been built by Statute Labour around 1806. It had been repaired and strengthened on a number of occasions since then and his view was that, whilst it was adequate for the existing traffic, it would need rebuilding if the volume of traffic increased. He felt that the proposed diversion and new

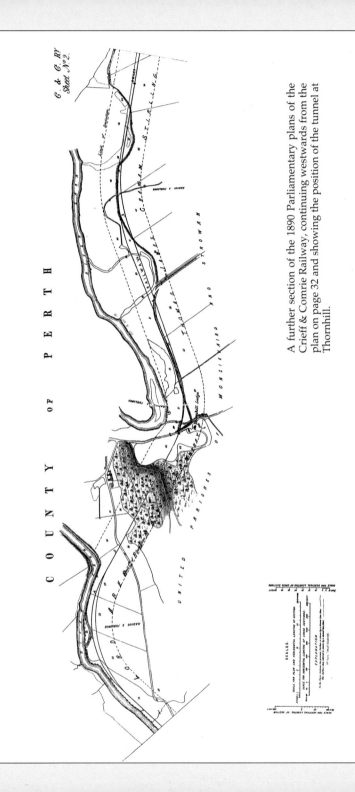

A further section of the 1890 Parliamentary plans of the Crieff & Comrie Railway, continuing westwards from the plan on page 32 and showing the position of the tunnel at Thornhill.

bridge would give a more direct access to the road on the south side of the river from any railway station built near Strowan.

In the end, the Select Committee rejected the proposals that the road should be diverted at the railway company's expense. They said that they had never known of a case in which the diversion of a road which was not interfered with in any way by a proposed railway had been ordered to be carried out at the expense of the railway company, and so they threw out all objections to the Bill.

As soon as the news was received in Comrie a congratulatory telegram was sent to Colonel Williamson who was staying at the Alexandra Hotel at Hyde Park Corner in London:

Comrie, 25/4/1890. People of Comrie highly delighted and in their name we send you congratulations and heartfelt thanks (Signed) John Comrie and William McIntyre.

The next day, after a night of festivities in the village, he received a telegram from his wife:

Comrie, 26/4/1890. Bonfire splendid. Crowds here all so enthusiastic and nice and grateful to you. Warm congratulations. (Signed) Selina.

The *Strathearn Herald* wrote in its issue of 1st May:

The people of Comrie have reason to be satisfied with the sweeping way they carried their Railway Bill before the Select Committee of the House of Commons. On every point the promoters of the Bill defeated their opponents and got all they could reasonably desire. It is to be regretted, more ways than one, that the opposers of the Bill should have been so ill advised as to have appeared before the Committee with so frivolous objections. From beginning to end their opposition was only wasting good money.

On Friday the inhabitants of Comrie rejoiced, as they had good reason to do, over their victory; but there was one regrettable incident in their joy, and that was, some of the more baser sort amongst them were so far left to themselves as to burn the effigy of Mr Graham Stirling of Strowan. Now, while we never sympathised with Mr Stirling in his opposition to the Bill, yet we granted, and we grant still, that he had quite a right to oppose it; nay more, in doing so, that did not show that he was opposed to a railway to Comrie. Mr Stirling, like all of us, has his own private rights to look after, and he is quite entitled to do so. Railway Companies are like all other Companies – very selfish concerns; and it is quite right for private individuals, without being opposed to the promotion of such Companies, to get all they can out of them. We should not have taken notice of this incident had it not been already the talk of the whole countryside, and utterly condemned by one and all. There are few men who have lived so long – more particularly landed proprietors – who are so highly respected and esteemed by the general community far and near as Thomas Graham Stirling of Strowan. His life-history is one that every man who understands what is moral and good will admire, and we have no hesitation in saying that the Comrie people have lowered themselves in the estimation of the community at large in allowing such a degrading act to be done upon an unoffending neighbour, simply because he thought it right to enforce what he conceived was his due. We are sure had Colonel Williamson, who has so successfully gained his point in London, and without whom the Comrie Railway would have been nowhere today, been present at these rejoicings, he would never have allowed so shameful a thing to be done on anyone, far less the old and much-respected proprietor of Strowan, who, we believe, is not capable of doing an ill turn to anybody.

Some people raised cautionary voices. Colonel Williamson received two letters from John Cameron of Edinburgh warning him that his estimate of the probable total outlay for the costs of land and construction was considerably under the mark.

His letters also say that the Caledonian Railway's suggestion of taking 50 per cent of the gross drawings was not unusual but as the North British Railway was only charging the West Highland Railway 45 per cent, the Caledonian ought not to charge more than that.

He suggested that the best way of raising the additional capital required would be to offer to pay the contractors in shares but this would cause the contractors to charge a higher price than if it was a cash contract. Failing this, Colonel Williamson and the other Directors would have to become personally responsible for the money to a bank or other capitalist.

A minor hiccup arose when the East Coast railway companies (Great Northern, North Eastern and North British) planned to appeal in the House of Lords for running powers (i.e. the right to run their own trains) over the new line. The Caledonian promised the promoters financial support up to a maximum of £250 if they opposed the appeal. In the event, nothing came of the proposal and construction of the line went ahead.

And what became of the objections?

In spite of various petitions over the years, the railway company never did build a station or siding at Thornhill.

Following Thomas Graham Stirling's failure to have the road in front of his mansion diverted at the railway company's expense, the matter lapsed for many years. Thomas Graham Stirling himself died in 1896 at the age of 85 and was buried in the churchyard at Strowan, within sight of his old house.

In time the estate passed out of the family's hands and is now owned by the Melville family. Subsequently Major Cox, the father-in law of the present owner, Major Mike Melville, gave land in exchange for greater privacy; the road was diverted and in 1971 a new bridge was built more or less on the site of Thomas Graham Stirling's proposed diversion. This is the present road that connects the A85 with the 'south' road to Crieff near the Curroch Smiddy. Just south of Thornhill Lodge it crosses the west portal of the tunnel through the Monument Hill.

The old Strowan House was demolished in the 1970s and a new house was built nearby. Portions of the old house remain as outbuildings.

But the old, decrepit bridge over the Earn at Strowan had the last laugh! In spite of its apparent weaknesses it survived intact until a major flood in the 1990s brought down one of its piers and the ruins had to be demolished. It thus outlived both the old house and the railway.

Chapter Four

Building the Crieff & Comrie Railway

The Engineer, Mr John Young, lost no time in preparing all the necessary plans and specifications and advertising for contractors. The following were successful:

Civil Engineering:	G. Mackay & Son, Broughty Ferry
Steel Rails:	Cammell & Sons, Sheffield
Cast Iron Chairs:	McFarlane, Strang & Co., Glasgow
Steel Fishplates:	Hurst & Co., Glasgow
Chair Spikes & Bolts:	P. & W. McLellan, Glasgow
Sleepers:	Bruce & Co., Glasgow
Oak Keys:	P. Sinclair & Co., Perth

The total length of the new line was 5 miles 7 furlongs and 5.2 chains, almost the same as the line surveyed 25 years earlier by Thomas Bouch. However, Thomas Bouch's original plan had considerably heavier gradients including a 300 yard tunnel. The new plan had a tunnel of only 90 yards length which passed between Trowan and the river. It was agreed to deviate the existing road to cross the tunnel about 20 yards from the Comrie end and run down its eastern side to rejoin the old road shortly before Thornhill Lodge; this was partly so that horses on the road would not be alarmed by the sudden appearance of a train from the nearby tunnel mouth.

The existing terminal station at Crieff would have to be rebuilt as a through station with increased facilities now that the railway was being extended westwards. The Caledonian Directors now remembered that, way back in 1865, the Scottish Central Railway (which it had since absorbed) had authorised itself to subscribe £20,000 to the Crieff & Comrie Railway Company of that year. They suggested to their solicitor that this long-forgotten £20,000 should now be brought back into capital account and the expenses of remodelling the station should be charged against it.

This was an accounting manoeuvre which would capitalise the remodelling expenses instead of charging them against their current year's profits. Their solicitor's reply is not recorded but the principle was perfectly legal.

Mr Buchan of Dundee was appointed valuer for the lands to be taken from Lord Abercrombie and Mr Graham Stirling agreed to accept him as regards his own land at Strowan. On 17th January, 1891 the *Strathearn Herald* reported a Dundee newspaper paper as saying that Messrs G. Mackay & Son, Broughty Ferry, had secured the contract for the construction of the Crieff & Comrie Railway at a cost of £22,000. The contractors were arranging to break ground at an early date and the new railway would afford them work for a considerable number of years.

That was a very prophetic comment!

At the same time Mr Shaw was writing to the Caledonian's Traffic Department, urging them to start the remodelling of Crieff station urgently so that Mackay & Son could be given facilities.

The ceremony of Cutting the First Turf of the Crieff & Comrie Railway. Performed at South Laggan Park, Comrie on 13th February, 1891 by the Hon. Mrs Williamson, wife of the Chairman of the company, Colonel Williamson.   *W. Gardiner*

The wheelbarrow and ceremonial spade used by the Hon. Mrs Williamson at the ceremony of Cutting the First Turf, 13th February, 1891.   *W. Gardiner*

A committee of ladies became actively engaged raising funds for the purchase of a barrow and silver spade to be used in cutting the first sod of the railway. Their fundraising must have gone well because Mr Nicol Rennie, a jeweller of Drummond Street, Comrie, was commissioned to supply a silver spade to be used by the Hon. Mrs Williamson of Lawers when lifting the first turf of the railway. At the same time, arrangements were also made to have a public procession during the day, a luncheon in the afternoon and a social gathering in the evening.

On 7th February, 1891 the *Strathearn Herald* was pleased to report that the spade and barrow to be used by the Hon. Mrs Williamson of Lawers when lifting the first turf of the Crieff & Comrie Railway on the 13th February were now to be seen in the shop window of Mr Crerar, wine merchant in Dunira Street, Comrie.

The wheelbarrow was made of polished mahogany, the handles and corners being beautifully mounted burnished brass. It was manufactured by Messrs Stewart & Macfarlane, joiners of Perth. The blade of the spade was made of sterling silver and weighed over 20 ounces. The handle was made of black ebony and was elaborately carved.

The forthcoming ceremony of cutting the first turf of the new railway was well advertised locally:

The Directors of the Crieff and Comrie Railway Company request and invite the Shareholders and their friends to be present at the ceremony of Cutting the First Turf of the Railway at Comrie on Friday the 13th February at One o'clock pm.

Luncheon at 2.30 pm in the Public Hall, Comrie. Tickets, 3s. 6d., to be had on application to P. Brough, Dundas House, Comrie.

The ceremony itself was advertised as follows:

CRIEFF AND COMRIE RAILWAY
CUTTING OF THE FIRST TURF ON FRIDAY 13TH FEBRUARY 1890

General Meeting, Public Hall, Comrie at Twelve mid-day.
Procession formed by Sergeant Burnett at 12.15 pm.

ORDER OF PROCESSION:
Crieff Instrumental Band, under the leadership of Mr J. Wilson and playing 'The Battlefields of Scotland'
Comrie Boy's Brigade
Comrie Schoolchildren carrying bannerettes, and under the charge of Mr Gibson, schoolmaster, and his assistants
Working Men of Comrie and District, preceded by a piper
Inhabitants of Comrie, composed of men and women
A lorry carrying the silver spade and the barrow with which the ceremony of cutting the turf was to be performed
Party of six navvies, attired in working garb and wheeling barrows
St Fillans Curling Club, carrying brooms
Lawers and Comrie Curling Club (all the members wearing medals won by the Club)
Monzievaird Curling Club
St Kessac's Lodge of Freemasons, No 269, Comrie, headed by Captain Dundas, RWM
St John's Lodge of Freemasons, No 92, Muthill headed by Rev. J. Leslie, RWM
St Michael's Lodge of Freemasons, No 38, Crieff

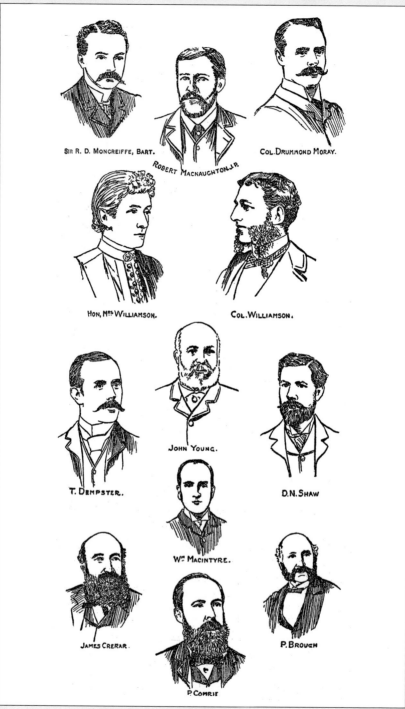

Portraits of Crieff & Comrie Railway personalities, *Perthshire Advertiser* 1893.

Crieff Town Council headed by Provost MacGregor and Bailies Adie and Cochrane
Lord-Provost Wilson, Perth
The Directors and Officers of the Crieff & Comrie Railway Company:
> Colonel D. R. Williamson of Lawers
> Colonel Drummond Moray of Blair-Drummond
> R. MacNaughtan, Esq. of Cowden
> Mr Peter Brough, Comrie
> Mr James Crerar, merchant
> Mr W. McIntyre, draper
> Mr P. Comrie, joiner
> Mr D.N. Shaw, Perth, Secretary to the Company
> Mr T. Dempster, Perth, Solicitor to the Company
> Mr J. Young, Perth, Engineer to the Company

Crieff Fire Brigade in uniform, with fire engines drawn by four horses
The rear of the procession to be brought up by another lorry filled with tools to be used
in connection with the construction of the railway.
Arrival at South Laggan Park, Comrie, at 12.45 pm.
Act of Parliament quoted, and a few remarks by the Provisional Chairman of the Crieff
and Comrie Railway Company.
Prayer will be offered up by the Rev. J. Campbell, minister of Monzievaird.

CEREMONY OF CUTTING THE FIRST TURF

by the Honourable Mrs Williamson of Lawers in South Laggan Park at 1 pm.
Luncheon in the Public Hall, Comrie, at 2.30 pm, when a few toasts will be proposed.
Tickets 3s. 6d. each
Social and Musical Entertainment in the Public Hall, Comrie, at 7 pm.
Colonel Williamson, Chairman
Admission: 6d. and 3d.

Bonfire at Tomperran, Lawers, and General Illuminations,
Full Blaze at 10 pm.

'GOD SAVE THE QUEEN AND OUR RAILWAY'

When the great day arrived the *Strathearn Herald* reported that:

Mrs Williamson then proceeded to the appointed spot, lifted the turf with the spade,
and placed it on the wheelbarrow, adding two spadefuls of earth. She then wheeled the
barrow along a plank to the centre of the enclosure where she deposited the contents.
Thereafter she turned about and, in real workmanlike fashion, pulled the barrow back
to where she had started and curtsied, amid tremendous cheering. Mrs Williamson then
said - 'I have to declare the first turf of the railway cut and the railway work begun'.
From the Public Hall to the park at the east end of the village, the streets were densely
crowded and loud cheering ever and anon greeted the processionists. On arriving at the
park where the ceremony was to take place, the different bodies that formed the
procession filed into the arena set apart for the event of the day. An immense concourse
of people had assembled with the schoolchildren and the Boys' Brigade ranged round
the inner circle, and the Masons and others behind.
In the South Laggan Park a space had been enclosed for the convenience of people
taking part in the ceremony. A marquee, decorated with evergreens, had been erected
for ladies. During the forenoon some thousands of people from the entire district round
crowded in to witness the ceremony and the streets were thronged with holidaymakers.

Large posters had been printed advertising the Social Entertainment to be held in the Public Hall on Friday evening, 13th February, at 7 o'clock. They advertised that songs, recitations and addresses would be given by ladies and gentlemen who had kindly consented to give their services on the occasion.

Entertainment was provided by the Misses Dewar and Steele, piano duettists, and lady singers who included Mrs Fitzgerald and Mrs Kelsall, both of Crieff, and Miss MacNaughtan of Cowden. Male singers included Messrs Roy, Main and Dempster. The programme also included a 'Song without Words' by Miss Tottie and a zither solo by Miss Block. The accompanists were Miss McCowan of Crieff and Miss Steele of Perth.

Shortly after the close of the concert the Hon. Mrs Williamson, in the presence of a large crowd, lit a huge bonfire composed of upwards of 100 loads of wood and other combustible materials on the top of Tomperran Hill. It was reported that the bonfire lighted up the country for miles around. In the course of the evening, rockets were fired and lime-lights were displayed in every part of the village. There was a very large display of Chinese lanterns and candles, the whole buildings in the village being illuminated.

The dance arranged by the young men to wind up the proceedings on the 13th was highly successful. About 50 couples were present and, aided by Mr McLean's Quadrille Band from Perth, they enjoyed themselves to the utmost. The Committee made a profit of £2, of which they gave £1 to the Hall Fund and 10s. each to the Reading Room and the Street Lighting Funds.

Celebrations also took place at St Fillans where a large bonfire was lit on the top of Crockmadt Hill.

In spite of having earlier objected to the railway's proposals, Crieff Town Council not only accepted an invitation to attend the new railway's opening ceremony at Comrie but also declared a Public General Holiday and recommended that all shops and places of business should close for the day to celebrate the coming of the railway, as per the following announcement:

PUBLIC HOLIDAY

The Magistrates and Commissioners of the Burgh of Crieff have fixed Friday the 13th inst. as a Close Holiday within the Burgh, in celebration of the cutting of the first turf of the Crieff & Comrie Railway, and recommend that all shops and places of business be closed on that day.

(signed) Wm France, Town Clerk.

The *Strathearn Herald* remarked, rather sourly, that whilst this was put as only a 'recommendation', everyone knew that it was tantamount to an instruction and they did not think it fair that the civic authorities should go off to Comrie to enjoy themselves at public expense and, at the same time, to expect local businesses to lose a whole day's trading. This seems to have caused a great deal of conscience-searching amongst the members of the Town Council and eventually they agreed to meet the cost of their outing from their own pockets.

The celebrations themselves were a huge success and were reported by the *Strathearn Herald* at great length:

Yesterday will long live in the memory of the inhabitants of Comrie and Upper Strathearn, and all who witnessed the interesting ceremonial and its attendant proceedings, as a red-letter day in the annals of the 'Earthquake City'.* The whole of the village and surrounding district were quite 'en fete' for the auspicious occasion. A general holiday was observed not only in the district, but in Crieff and Muthill, the result being that there were about 4,000 people present. Of that number a very large proportion were from Crieff - many brakes and carriages being run to and from Comrie during the day; whilst hundreds walked on foot - it being the general remark that never before were so many people seen on the road between Crieff and Comrie. The people of Comrie were of course in a very jubilant mood, and all vied with each other in displaying their joy and enthusiasm over this great event in their history. Almost every building was less or more decorated with bunting and flags in a most effective fashion, the result being that the village presented a very gay appearance. The weather, fortunately, was of a favourable character, which enabled the spectators to enjoy the day's proceedings with comparative comfort.

The decorations, as stated above, were of the most elaborate character, nearly every house having its own particular display of bunting. At the south end of the Bridge of Ross the roadway was spanned by a tastefully-designed arch, made with evergreens and fir trees, the arch being surmounted with pretty coloured flags. In Burrell Street the houses of Craigforth, Turleum View, Rose Cottage and Wood View were tastefully decorated with gaily-coloured bunting, and a banner floated over the Public Hall.

At the corner of Burrell Street the house and shop of Mr McCulloch, baker, was adorned with flags and a line of evergreens; while a line of flags crossed the roadway leading to Glenlednock. The shop of Mrs Drummond adjoining was also nicely decorated.

In Dundas Street, amongst the most artistic displays were those over the premises occupied by Mr Mellis, watchmaker, and Mr Roy, carrier; while from one house in the same street flags were displayed with the mottoes 'Good Luck' and 'Success'.

In Dunira Street, some of the houses and business premises were very tastefully decorated. Conspicuous amongst these was the ingenuity shown in the decoration over the shops occupied by Mr John Comrie, merchant; Mr Crerar, merchant; Mr Robertson, seedsman; and Mr P. Davidson, game-dealer. Mr Comrie's shop front was tastefully adorned with scarlet cloth, nicely arranged, and had the Royal Arms and a portrait of Her Majesty conspicuously displayed. A line of flags also spanned the street from Dundas House to the smithy opposite. Waving over Mr Crerar's premises, too, was a large banner, while his house was nicely set out with bunting and holly. Flags also adorned the shop of Mr Brough and other houses adjoining.

In Drummond Street immense masses of bunting were displayed. Over the shop of Mr Drummond, bookseller, was the motto 'Union is Railway Strength'; while on the opposite side, the shop of Mr McIntyre, draper, was effectively adorned with coloured bunting. Stretching across the street, opposite Mr Dinnie's, cabinetmaker, was a line of pretty flags, some of them with mottoes. Another line of streamers spanned the road a little further east, one bearing these words - 'All you that have cash to spare, take stock in the Comrie Railway'. A local shoemaker had over his premises the words, worked out in leaves - 'Nothing like leather'. One of the most effectively decorated buildings was the Commercial Hotel (Mrs McNeil's), which was elaborately decorated with evergreens, Chinese lanterns, bannerettes, a portrait of the Queen, and a mass of gay bunting, in the centre of which was conspicuous the words, 'Success to our Railway'. Over the premises of Messrs Comrie, joiners, was a similar motto. The public road from Drummond Street, onward to Lawers, was decorated at intervals with gaily-coloured flags and bunting. It was also reported that the Commercial Bank displayed the Union Jack and other banners.

In Dalginross and vicinity nearly every house displayed bunting, the most tasteful design being shown at Rosebank; while the Bridgend Hotel was decorated with flags, from each point of vantage, and in centre of bunting had the words 'Success to our Railway'.

---

* Comrie lies on the geological Highland Fault and over the centuries it has recorded more earth tremors than any other place in Britain. For this reason it is known locally as 'Earthquake City' or 'The Shaky Toun'.

The first ordinary meeting of shareholders took place just over a year later, on 4th March, 1891. It was held in the Public Hall, Comrie, and was attended by the Directors, Secretary, and around 50 shareholders. The Chairman, Colonel Williamson, reported that £28,694 of the authorised capital of £45,000 had now been subscribed and that the total undertaking was expected to cost around £39,000. Six Directors and a number of other gentlemen had travelled to London to be questioned by the Parliamentary Committee in the course of getting the Railway Bill through Parliament and they had been reimbursed moderate expenses for their trouble. Their railway had concluded a working agreement with the Caledonian company whereby the latter would take 50 per cent of the gross receipts and also charge a perpetual rent of £150 per year for the use of the new station that was being built at Crieff.

As regards their position with the various landlords along the course of the line, they had firstly had to deal with three house-owners in Crieff and had practically concluded arrangements with them to the company's advantage. Unfortunately, they were still experiencing difficulties in dealing with Mr Hunter's glebe at Crieff but this should be concluded shortly.

The Revd John Hunter, minister of the West Parish Church in Crieff, had a four-acre glebe beside the Bridge of Turret that had been gifted by Sir Patrick Murray. He wanted a total of £50 compensation for the railway taking a small part of his glebe (⅕ acre). The railway company offered him £4 for land and £6 for everything else (loss of amenity, etc.), total £10, and that seems to have been the end of the matter.

More seriously, the Crieff Town Council wanted a great deal of money for the section of the Town Meadow required by the railway and they rejected the Directors' offer of arbitration.

The Town Council initially claimed that the meadow belonged to the town but investigations proved that the meadow actually belonged to Lord Willoughby and the feuars of Crieff had only a right of servitude over it – a right to use it as a bleaching green. The Council next formed a committee to ascertain the town's rights over the green and to try to arrange a settlement with Lord Willoughby and the railway company. The Town Council wanted £900 for the land but the Directors offered only £750. Stalemate ensued and the Council said it would petition the House of Lords against the Bill being passed.

The *Strathearn Herald*, never a friend of the Council, wrote scathingly about their naiveté, firstly in making their objections too late to be considered by the Commons Select Committee and, secondly, in not realising that the cost of making an appeal to the Lords would far outweigh any increased compensation they might be awarded. In the event, the Council grudgingly accepted the railway company's offer.

Lord Willoughby behaved very generously and sold his land at the price put on it by the company's Engineer; moreover he agreed to take the value of his land in shares in the company, which amounted to £1,650. Sir Patrick Keith Murray was even more generous and sold his land to the company at around £55 per acre although it was valued at £130 per acre. Colonel Williamson himself sold his land at less than £60 per acre although, like Sir Patrick's, its commercial value was £130 per acre.

This left Lord Abercrombie and Mr Graham Stirling who entered into arbitration for the value of their land. Prohibition to place a foot on either the Abercrombie or Strowan estates was threatened by lawyer-factors unless the Directors gave personal security for a large sum of money in case it might be required. In all other cases where the buffer of a lawyer-factor was not involved, settlements were made without delay or expense.

Contracts had been placed to a value of £30,188 and work on building the line had already commenced close to the Turret. The date specified for the completion of the line was 13th July, 1892 but it was hoped that the work would be finished by 1st July of that year.

The first shareholders' meeting wholeheartedly approved of the situation and unanimously re-elected the existing Board of Directors.

In 1891 Colonel Williamson had built a public entertainments hall (now the Masonic Hall) in Comrie for the benefit of the local residents. He named it the 'David and Selina Hall' after his wife and himself and it now became the venue for the half-yearly meetings of the railway company. At the half-yearly meeting held on Wednesday 26th August, 1891 he reported that up to 9th August they had disposed of 5,254 shares at £5 each, realising £26,270. Lord Willoughby had agreed to take the value of his land in shares (£1,650) and so had Sir Patrick Keith Murray (£617). With further investments since that date the capital raised was now £28,562. The contract for the formation and materials of the line now amounted to £30,188. He said that the company wanted another £10,000 *and he intended to get it!*

The number of shareholders was now 440 and arrears on calls were only £85. The company had taken out a private loan of £4,000 which was guaranteed by the Directors; this was because there would otherwise have been a delay in starting construction. The money was put at the disposal of the arbiters for the lands to be taken from Lord Abercrombie and Mr Graham Stirling.

Colonel Williamson also paid compliments to the conduct of the navvies, of whom there were currently 200 employed. He said that ample provision had been made by the contractor for their accommodation at various parts along the route.

The Engineer's report mentioned that a 6 ft x 6 ft heading was being driven through the tunnel and was being continually worked night and day by squads of navvies through very hard and splintery rock. Until this was completed the spoil from the eastern part of the line could not be taken through for use in embankments on the western part by the Carse of Trowan Farm. The materials in the various cuttings were generally composed of boulder clay with stratas of sand or gravel. Mr J.W. Moncur of Perth was the resident engineer.

An unfortunate accident had occurred the previous day when Patrick O'Donnell, a navvy aged about 50, was killed when undermining the side of an embankment in a cutting on the north west side of Sir David Baird's monument. Around two tons of material collapsed onto him; he was pulled out alive but died shortly afterwards from a fractured skull.

Meanwhile the railway was inspiring local poets to take up their pens. The following poem appeared in the *Alichmore Trumpet* on 31st October, 1891:

The Crieff & Comrie Railway
(Sung to the Air of 'Braes o' Mar')

Standing on the Sauchie Road
I see the Comrie Railway,
The navvies they are working hard,
And they work hard and sairly.
The bogies they ply down the line,
The gaffers crying all the time;
Come young and auld, the day is fine,
And see the Comrie Railway.

The first obstruction in the way
Was that cuttin' thro' the Sauchie Brae;
But I think we'll all agree to say
They'll soon complete the Railway.

The navvies work wi' richt guid will,
The bogies they do quickly fill;
You'll never catch them standin' still
Upon the Comrie Railway.

The Laird of Strowan he opposed
The Bill, when in the House o' Lords,
But the Colonel he put in his nose
And fair surprised Graham-Stirling.

The Laird says he'll never rest;
He declares he'll turn the east from west,
But he may lie down and tak' a rest,
For he'll never stop the Railway.

Three cheers for Colonel Williamson,
For he's worked late and early;
If it hadna' been for that brave man
We would never ha' seen the Railway.

The Comrie folk they might be proud
For he's done them a lot of good;
He was the only man that stood
In favour of the Railway.

The *Alichmore Trumpet* appears to have been a generally satirical paper which was published in Crieff and owned by a body known as F.M.H.A.H.A.

Already money was running short and as early as 21st October, 1891 Colonel Williamson had had yet another meeting with Mr Bolton, the Chairman of the Caledonian Railway, to ask if the Caledonian would make a subscription towards completing the Crieff & Comrie Railway.

Mr Bolton's reply was uncompromising: he reiterated that his Board was unanimously against providing any money in aid of the undertaking and he could hold out no hope of them altering their decision. Once again the company was on its own!

The next half-yearly meeting of shareholders took place in February 1892. Besides the Directors and Secretary, around 40 to 50 shareholders were reported as being present.

Colonel Williamson opened the meeting by reiterating that the contractor was bound by the terms of his contract to finish the line by 13th July next and that he should have no reason for not finishing the line by that date. The contractor had always had possession of the ground whenever he wanted it and his accounts had always been paid on the very day that he had presented them.

Allowing for calls in arrears, which he had every confidence would be made good, the capital so far subscribed was now £33,115. Unfortunately, costs had escalated since the last meeting and it was now likely that the railway would cost at least £42,000. The Directors had received a private loan of £4,000 which they had personally guaranteed but this had now been reduced to £3,000. He himself did not expect, and would not accept, any fee for his services as Chairman.

He went on to say that he hoped this would be their last half-yearly meeting before the line was opened. Out of a total length of 5 miles 7 furlongs and 5 chains, approximately 3½ miles had already been made including more than two-thirds of the 90 yards-long tunnel at the Monument Hill.

The monies spent on acquiring the land were as follows (to the nearest pound)

Lord Willoughby	3.4 acres	£1,650	(taken in shares)
Sir Keith Murray	11.6 acres	£617	
Mr Graham Stirling	11.7 acres	£2,325	
Col Williamson	7.2 acres	£400	
Ferntower	7.2 acres	£600	(approx)
Houses in Crieff		£800	(approx)

making a total of around £6,400.

Colonel Williamson went on to say, in an obvious sideswipe at his long-time friend Thomas Graham Stirling, that he regretted very much that the company had sometimes had to pay four times as much for one acre of land as they had to pay for another acre of equal quality. On a more cheerful note, he remarked that their little company had been the means of giving Crieff a beautiful new station a year or two earlier than they would otherwise have had it.

In conclusion, he pointed out that the subscribed capital was still around £9,000 short of the amount required to finish the railway in its entirety. Whilst the Directors did not like to ask people for an extra £100 or £500, he was sure that when people realised that the railway was for the good not only of the immediate neighbourhood but for the good of the country as a whole, they would contribute and that a large proportion of the money would be obtained by the sale of ordinary shares.

Two other interesting matters were raised at that meeting. One was that Mr S. Campbell, a farmer of Lochalour, asked if there was any proposal to have a siding at Thornhill. Colonel Williamson replied that the matter had been under the consideration of the Directors that very day and, whilst he could not give him a definite answer at present, one would be sent to him through the Secretary.

The second interesting matter was that Mr Peter Brough had received from Mr Archibald Kay, an expatriate of Blairinroar now living in Ballarat, Victoria,

Australia, a gift of a ton of oxide of iron paint for use in painting the carriages and wagons of the new railway.

A momentous event happened on 23rd March, 1892 when Colonel Williamson lit the last fuse in the tunnel workings and sunlight shone through for the very first time. Appropriately, the Colonel himself was the first to pass through the opening and he is said to have treated the workmen very handsomely.

There was still a considerable amount of work to be done before the line was completed but now at least the contractor could transfer spoil from the eastern end of the line to build the embankment on the west side.

Yet another attempt to get the Caledonian to help with finances was made in June 1892 when Colonel Williamson again wrote to their Directors, pointing out that the new railway was now three-quarters finished and asking for around £9,000 to complete the line. His request was refused point-blank.

Still the promoters persevered and a month later Mr Shaw again asked the Caledonian Directors to receive a deputation. The Caley's Secretary was instructed to ask them what business they were upon, whereupon nothing more was heard of it. Their only concession was to grant Colonel Williamson a free pass over their lines between Crieff and Glasgow, Edinburgh and Dundee.

Subsequently this facility was granted to all the Directors of the new railway and, in addition, a Joint Committee was set up comprising Lord Breadalbane and Mr Bruiten from the Caledonian and Colonel Williamson and Mr Crerar from the Crieff & Comrie Railway. One of their duties would be to fix the rates to be charged for traffic on the new line.

The next half-yearly meeting was held on 31st August, 1892 but, apart from the Directors and officers of the company, only about a dozen shareholders attended.

On this occasion news of progress on the line was not good and Colonel Williamson made a verbal attack on the contractors, Mackay & Son. Under the terms of the contract the line should have been ready for opening on 13th July, five weeks ago, but the project was running far behind schedule.

Colonel Williamson said that during the long period of 40 years he had built a large number of houses and cottages, had made roads, put up perhaps 30 or 40 miles of fencing, filled up ponds, and planted considerably, and except on one occasion no contractor had ever failed to keep faith with him, so far as the time of finishing his work was concerned. He admitted that those contractors were all local men, connected with the district. Seing that those small contractors were able to fulfil their engagements to the very day, he expected that a man in the position of their contractor (Mr Mackay) would have been able to finish this much more important work on time. He felt that the contractor had not been a very good bargain and perhaps if they had accepted a higher offer the railway might have been finished on time

He went on to say that the most important subject the shareholders had to deal with was the lack of sufficient capital to finish the line. According to the accounts they now had a capital of £35,225 which was likely to increase shortly to £35,585. If they had only £36,000 to build a railway which was to cost £45,000, there would be a deficiency of £9,000. The Directors were prepared to invest another £1,000 of their own money if the shareholders would come up with the other £8,000.

He was hoping that various gentlemen interested in the locality and personal friends of his own might contribute more capital and he urged existing shareholders to do their utmost to gain additional shareholders. He also said that he had taken a great deal of trouble to ascertain the amount of traffic that passed along the road between Crieff and Comrie, and he had come to the conclusion that there was no road in Scotland that had the same amount of traffic upon it; therefore he felt satisfied that the railway would pay a very good dividend indeed. He assured the meeting that the Directors would do everything in their power to complete the railway with the utmost economy.

The Engineer, Mr Young, reported that 4½ miles of the railway had been roughly completed to formation level. All the bridges were now completed excepting the parapets, and the bridges over the burn at Thornhill and Balmenoch were ready for the steelwork. The bridge at King Street, Crieff, would be opened for traffic in a few days time and the culvert over the Balmenoch Burn was in progress of construction. The tunnel, which had been substituted for retaining walls and an open cutting at Drummawhandie, Crieff, was now finished, excepting the wing walls, and the earth was being filled on top of the arch to bring the ground to its original surface. The tunnel at Trowan had been driven to its full length and the brick lining was being proceeded with. The open cutting at the north end of this tunnel was being pushed forward and a connection through the tunnel would be made in a few weeks, when it was expected that greater progress would be made with the embankment towards Comrie. The road diversion at Thornhill was finished and open for traffic. All the permanent way materials were now supplied, excepting part of the chairs and sleepers, and these were being brought to the works as required. A considerable portion of the permanent way had been laid and ballasted. The foundations of the offices at Comrie station had been completed and the woodwork was about ready for erecting.

To date, £30,211 had been spent on the project and a further £17,053 was still to be spent. This made a total of £47,264, of which around £10,000 would have to be paid in the next six months. £14,862 of the contract price of £30,188 was still outstanding and was included in these figures.

As usual the Colonel had been indefatigable in firing off letters to everyone concerned. From writing nine letters in 1891 he had gone on to write 34 in 1892 and no less than 73 in 1893. Most of these were directed to the Secretary, Mr D.N. Shaw; the contractors, Mackay & Son; the engineer, John Young and to Major-General Hutchinson, the Board of Trade officer who was to inspect the line before it could commence operations. Many of the 1892 letters complained about delays in construction and those in 1893 about the contractor's charges.

At the half-yearly meeting held on 28th February, 1893 the Engineer reported that about 5½ miles of the railway was now completed to formation width and level, and ready for the soiling and dressing of the slopes. Three and a half miles of the track were completed and a further mile was laid ready for ballasting. All the culverts and bridges were completed, as were the tunnels at Crieff and Trowan. The long embankment through the lands of Strowan and Lawers was far advanced and all that was required to complete the works of the main line was 1,100 lineal yards to be embanked and the track laid on it.

A plan dated 20th February, 1890 of the new Crieff station shows approach roads laid at a gradient of 1 in 20 from King Street. The eastbound platform shows (from west) Booking Office, Station Master, Parcels, Ladies 2nd Class, Entrance, Ladies 1st Class, Gents 1st Class, General Waiting Room, Porters. The same layout was repeated on the opposite platform but with no booking office and with the ticket collector's office opposite the station master's office. All the buildings were covered by a verandah with a cab stand outside. The width of the cab stand was 30 feet and the approach roadway was 25 feet wide. The level crossing at Duchlage Street had been replaced by a new bridge.

In February 1893 the buildings at Comrie station were ready to be painted whilst work on the sidings, loading banks and station equipment was well advanced. An 1892 plan of the station shows a single platform containing offices, opposite to which was a sheep loading bank. The layout of the sidings included a goods shed at the western end of another loading bank which had a cattle pen at the Crieff end. Adjacent to the passenger platform at the eastern end was a horse loading bank whilst a small engine shed was located at the Crieff end of a triangular set of tracks on which locomotives could be turned for their return journey to Crieff.

Notwithstanding the severe weather that had recently been experienced, the works had made fair progress and were being pushed forward with the utmost rigour to have the line completed and opened at the earliest possible date.

Unfortunately, costs were soaring. The cost of the land purchased had increased to £9,265 and the construction of the line, including engineering work, had so far amounted to £28,738. Together with other necessary expenses incidental to obtaining their Act, the total amount expended on the unfinished railway had been £43,915 and the likely final cost was now £48,000.

Capital received from the share issue had been £36,713 so the Directors had been forced to raise money by other means. The contractors had accepted payment of £1,460 in Lloyd's bonds and the Directors had personally guaranteed an overdraft of £6,078 with the Clydesdale Bank

By early 1893 the estimated cost of completing the railway had risen to £55,000 and an Extraordinary General Meeting was held in the Public Hall in Comrie. The Directors asked for powers to raise up to a further £15,000 by issuing debentures upon mortgage of the undertaking because all their money had been spent and they themselves had become personally liable for the company's debts. Their request was agreed to.

However, not everything was doom and gloom. The following report appeared in the *Strathearn Herald* on 17th May:

THE LINE NEARLY COMPLETED

The construction of this line is now nearing completion. On Wednesday last the embankments at either end were joined near Comrie, and temporary rails laid down which, with the most of the permanent way already laid, enabled the contractor's engines to pass over the entire length of the line from Crieff to Comrie. A large number of the inhabitants of Comrie turned out to see the first engine steaming into the station. It was generally known in the beginning of the week that the banks were to be met on Wednesday. Numerous stories were circulated in connection with the great event. A local trader had promised the engine driver a pint of whisky if he would run his engine into the station on the day fixed. This pint rapidly increased until it had reached a half-barrel, and from that to three barrels of beer and a barrel of whisky. Whether this had anything to do with the large turnout of spectators, we will not judge. Precisely at six o'clock the engine, decorated with flags and evergreens, hove in sight, and as it drew nearer it was observed that Colonel Williamson, Chairman of the Company, along with other gentlemen, were the occupants of the first train to Comrie. As the Colonel was recognised, loud cheers were raised and cries for a speech. The Colonel addressed those present, and thanked the workmen who had laboured at the making of the railway with their brawny arms, those who had done the thinking part, those who had put their hands in their pockets, and the ladies who had done a great deal towards the forwarding of the scheme. He then presented Robert Cameron and Alexander McIntyre with a pound note each, their reward for sticking to their work at the railway since its commencement. The engine driver was also presented with a note for guiding the first train to Comrie. Mr. Cameron having thanked the Colonel for his kindness, Mr Mackay, the contractor for the line, also made a short speech, and assured the inhabitants that he would have the line ready for traffic by 1st June. On the motion of Colonel Williamson, three hearty cheers were given for Mr Mackay. The engines then steamed out of the station on their way to Crieff, amid the cheers of the crowd.

A few days later an engine hauling three coaches and a large carriage truck passed slowly over the line. It conveyed officials of the Caledonian Railway and other interested parties whose purpose was to carry out a minute inspection of the railway and its engineering works before it was formally inspected by the Board of Trade. After doing so they lunched at McNeil's Commercial Hotel in Comrie before returning to Crieff.

The formal inspection of the line on behalf of the Board of Trade was made by Major-General Hutchinson on 29th May, 1893. Arriving at Crieff in a special train around 9 o'clock in the morning he was met by Colonel Williamson and the operating managers of the new railway and of the Caledonian.

After inspecting the signalling apparatus and points at Crieff and then the new station itself, Major-General Hutchinson and the officials boarded a special train and passed slowly down the line. They first of all made a detailed inspection of the King Street bridge, the tunnel under Burrell Street and Drummawhandie, the Sauchie Road bridge and finally the bridge over the River Turret. The latter was tested with a locomotive of more than 70 tons weight. The party then continued along the line, inspecting the various bridges and culverts, until they reached the tunnel at Baird's Monument, 90 yards long and the heaviest part of the work on the line. Here a very careful examination was made of its interior before the party continued on their way along the Carse of Strowan, inspecting several more bridges on the way. On arrival at Comrie the station, signals and points were examined before Major-General Hutchinson expressed his general satisfaction with the railway and declared it ready for traffic.

The *Strathearn Herald* described the route of the line in the following terms:

> After leaving the station, the railway to Comrie passes through a deep cutting in Crieff Meadow on to Burrell Street where there is a tunnel 300 feet long. Thereafter, passing under Sauchie public road, which has been raised and diverted a few feet further west, a high embankment conducts the line on to the river Turret, where there is a substantial steel bridge with three spans, the largest being 54 feet from centre to centre of piers. The two main girders are each 54 feet long and 5 feet deep.

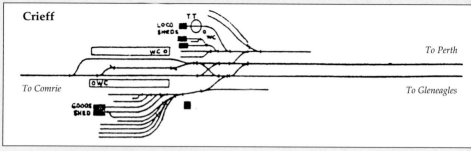

Crieff

To Perth

To Comrie

To Gleneagles

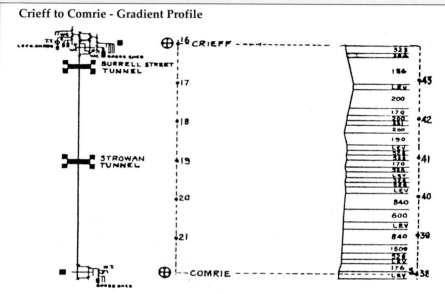

Crieff to Comrie - Gradient Profile

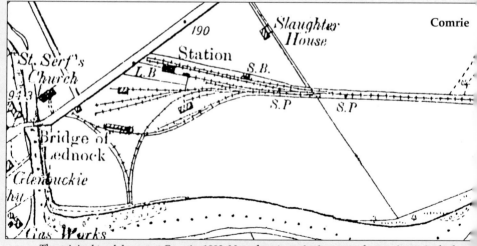

Comrie

The original track layout at Comrie, 1893. Note the triangular layout in the goods yard which was used for turning tender engines due to the absence of a turntable. The siding parallel to the platform line served a sheep-loading bank.

The line now enters upon the beautiful estate of Sir Patrick Keith Murray, Baronet of Ochtertyre, and runs almost in a parallel course with the river Earn. Speeding along for a mile or two, the most important and heaviest portion of the work of construction of the line is approached - namely the tunnel, 100 yards long, that passes through the haunch of the hill whereon Baird's Monument stands. At the west end of the tunnel there is a heavy open cutting, and the public road to Monzievaird had here to be diverted at considerable cost. Thereafter the line emerges on the open plain of the Carse of Strowan, along which it is carried on an embankment for nearly three miles, and close to the river embankment. The railway terminates at the east end of Comrie, near the Bridge of Lednock, upon ground belonging to Colonel Williamson. The heaviest gradient on the line is at the Crieff end where for some distance it is 1 in 156, falling towards Comrie.

The paper then concludes with a prophetic comment:

It only now requires one more link to complete the chain of direct communication between the Atlantic and German Oceans - from Oban to Dundee - the distance between Comrie and Lochearnhead, 14 or 15 miles, where the Callander & Oban railway passes, and the sooner, perhaps, that this is done the better it will be for the interests of the Comrie Railway shareholders.

The ceremonial opening of the Crieff and Comrie Railway took place on 1st July, 1893 and was reported in the *Strathearn Herald* as follows:

On Thursday last, the railway and also the new station at Crieff were opened for traffic. The day was happily all that could be wished, and not only the inhabitants of Comrie, but many Crieff people took advantage of a trip by the new route.

The first train left Crieff for Comrie about 6.30 am, it being thought advisable in the meantime to lodge the engines and carriages overnight at Crieff. On arrival at Comrie there was very little appearance of excitement over the auspicious event, only a very few of the inhabitants putting in an appearance to see the first train start for Crieff, where a large number awaited its arrival. Not till twelve o'clock noon was there any appearance of extra traffic. By the train which reaches Crieff from the south about that hour a large number of the Crieffites availed themselves of visiting the 'Earthquake City' by rail.

As a matter of course, Thursday was a red-letter day in the history of Comrie. Numerous banners were flying on both public and private buildings but, apart from this, there were little signs of outward decorations except on the handsome hotels belonging to Mrs McNeil in Drummond Street and Mrs Ferguson in Dalginross, where some little pains had been taken to show their outward rejoicing at the completion of so important an undertaking, fraught with so much benefit to the future of the village. In other directions the villagers were alive to the importance of the advent of railway communication. By twelve o'clock the shops and places of business were all shut and a half-holiday determined upon; and it could be seen that not only the young, but the genuine old villagers who seldom, under the old order of conveyance, cared to take a trip from home, were eagerly bent to have a first day's run by the iron horse to Crieff. Even our old friend - the Comrie coachman - whose craft was not only in danger, but gone altogether, was amongst the passengers by the 1.40 pm train, looking as happy and pleased like as if he was about to enter upon a fortune. Happy man! How we do admire his spirit. His loss is Comrie's gain. We need not say that, as a matter of course, no day's rejoicings among Comrie folk could be complete without the presence of the gallant Colonel of Lawers. Indeed, his absence from the scene of rejoicing up till midday was a matter of considerable anxiety and enquiry, if not amongst the Comrie people, at least amongst those in Crieff - for everyone in the 'Capital of Strathearn' expected to see the

A map of Crieff around the end of the 19th century. The old and new stations are in the centre.

gallant Colonel, not only with the first train, but mounted on the first engine in the morning. However, the Colonel, accompanied by the Hon. Mrs Williamson, turned up at midday just as the passenger traffic for the day was at its best.

The midday train from Comrie brought hundreds of the natives to Crieff by a new and hitherto untrodden way, and there is not the least doubt but that this new iron highway will be of great advantage to Comrie.

In point of fact, the first train to steam into Comrie station on that memorable morning comprised seven six-wheeled carriages hauled by 2-4-0 tender engine No. 467 (*see photograph*). She had been designed by the Caledonian's chief mechanical engineer, Benjamin Connor, built by the private locomotive-building firm of Dübs & Co. in 1875 and originally numbered 637 before being renumbered in the following year.

The *Strathearn Herald* goes on to give details of the train service provided on the line. The existing five daily trains each way between Crieff and the main line to the south at Crieff Junction (nowadays Gleneagles) now started from Comrie and there were four trains in the opposite direction. The two trains each way on the Crieff to Perth line also were re-scheduled to start from Comrie.

Times were as follows:

Comrie dep. 7.10, 8.20, 10.20 am, 1.40, 4.40 pm, all to Crieff Junction.
Also 10.20 am and 5.37 pm to Perth.
Arrivals were at 10.13 am (from the South and Perth, joined at Crieff), 12.15, 3.15 pm (from Crieff Jn) and 6.25 pm (4.05 pm from Glasgow).

There were also two arrivals from Perth. The 6.22 am from Stirling connected with overnight expresses from London to Glasgow and Edinburgh, leaving there at around 5.00 am and arriving at Comrie at 7.40 am. This meant that the post now arrived at Comrie at breakfast-time instead of at midday by coach. The running time allowed between Comrie and Crieff was 15 minutes with speed restrictions of 12 miles per hour on the sharpest curves.

The first train to arrive at Comrie station on 1st July, 1893. The locomotive is 2-4-0 No. 467, designed by Benjamin Connor and built by Dübs & Company in 1875. She was originally numbered 637 and was renumbered 467 in 1876.   *J. MacIntosh*

The newspaper was less enthusiastic about the appearance of the new station at Crieff:

The buildings are, like most other railway constructions, of wood and is, we believe, considered commodious enough for the traffic. While its situation is not the best for giving it that imposing look that might well be looked for, yet it must be confessed that the architect might have improved it greatly had he raised the elevation of the walls higher and lessened the size of the roofs. Viewed from King Street, the buildings have a very toy-like appearance at best. Perhaps, however, what is more important, the spaces allocated for cabs and carriages outside the buildings on either side are no better than at the old station and must, undoubtedly, ere long result in a demand for more room. It is to be feared that the Railway Company are penny wise and pound foolish in this respect. What they ought to have done - and what they will require to do ere long - was to have utilised the whole of their ground on the north side of the station and carry their main roadway out to Commissioner Street. Until this is done matters will neither be satisfactory nor safe for the general public. The new platforms are a decided improvement on the old ones. The arrival and departure platforms are each 700 feet in length, 300 feet on each side being covered with a verandah. The station buildings on both up and down lines are 180 feet long; while the platforms are 29 feet wide opposite the offices, and 15 feet at the ends. The offices are neat and commodious. The change of the site of the station necessitated the erection of new bridges at Duchlage Road and King Street - at the east and west end of the station buildings, the former costing about £2,000, while the whole works, including this bridge, is said to have cost about £14,000.

In December 1893 the Caledonian agreed to take on responsibility for the line's maintenance.

As early as January 1894 a petition was signed by farmers, graziers, merchants and others in the parish of Comrie and neighbourhood, asking for a better winter train service. The Caley refused to reinstate the summer service but referred the matter to their superintendent of the line, Mr Irvine Kempt, to meet their wishes as far as possible.

At the same time, on a more sociable note, their Traffic Committee granted Colonel Williamson the right to trap rabbits on the railway's embankments in return for a payment of 2s. 6d. per year.

Comrie in the late 19th century with the newly-built parish church of St Kessog in the foreground.   *Author's Collection*

Chapter Five

Colonel's Williamson's Testimonial

In appreciation of Colonel Williamson's efforts in bringing the railway to Comrie, a committee was formed to present him with a Testimonial at a cake and wine banquet which was held at the Public Hall on 20th September, 1893. The Committee comprised 28 gentlemen with Thomas Boston of Balmuick as Chairman, Mr H. Campbell, banker, as Treasurer and Mr J.P. Mitchell as Secretary.

Contributions were readily forthcoming and the committee soon raised the sum of £200. They decided to purchase three silver basins and an illuminated Address for the Colonel, along with a solid silver tea service for his lady.

The *Strathearn Herald* described the gifts as follows:

The presentation plate consisted of three pieces of silver-plate, a large and massive silver basin being the centre piece, with two smaller silver basins to match, all mounted on ebony pedestals. All are designed in an ornate French style of art, boldly and richly treated with shaped and masked edgings, and chased festoons of flowers and ornament carried all round above a base of flat fluting. The body of the large basin is divided into six extensive shields between masks and festoons. On all of these are engraved subjects executed by Mr Macgregor, jeweller, Perth, as follows:- (1) a view of Lawers House, showing the sylvan loveliness of the scene to admirable effect, with the fine mansion set in the midst; (2) a view of the new railway station at Comrie, with the train standing by, depicted with great minuteness and truth; (3) a finely-engraved portrait of the popular Laird of Lawers; (4) a portrait of the Hon. Mrs Williamson; (5) the full coat-of-arms of Robertson-Williamson of Lawers; and (6) the inscription as follows:
Presented to Colonel D.R. Williamson of Lawers, Chairman of the Crieff and Comrie Railway, by shareholders and others interested in the railway, in recognition of his invaluable services to the Company - 1st June 1893.
The present to the Hon. Mrs Williamson was, as already stated, a solid silver tea service of Indian design. The set, which is a most elegant and handsome one, consists of a large and very artistically chased tray, a teapot, sugar-basin, cream-pot and hot-water or claret jug. The whole are elaborately chased with Indian figures, especially the tray, which is a magnificent piece of art. The entire set is very neatly fitted with a cabinet of fine polished wood which, opening from the centre and the lid lifting upwards, shows the whole of the pieces nicely arranged. In the centre of the tray is the following inscription:
Presented to the Honourable Mrs Williamson by shareholders and others interested in the Crieff and Comrie Railway, in recognition of the great interest taken by her in this railway, and of the invaluable services rendered to the Company by her husband, Colonel D.R. Williamson of Lawers, 1st June 1893.

For the second time in less than four months the village went *en fete*. In the afternoon of the presentation the principal shops were shut and most of the shops and houses were beautifully decorated; while in the evening the houses were illuminated. The good people of Comrie were obviously intent on getting their money's-worth out of the decorations they had bought when the Railway Bill was passed in 1890!

The *Strathearn Herald* described the decorations in the following terms (abbreviated):

Not only were the shops and better class of houses tastefully adorned with bunting, etc., but even the poorest of the villagers showed their gratitude, as well as their regard, for the man who had done so much towards bringing prosperity to the community, by displaying from their humble dwellings a little bit of bunting or some flowers neatly disposed about their windows. The decorations were mainly confined to the principal thoroughfares of the village. All the way west from Lawers to Comrie, however, flags and other emblems of rejoicing could be seen floating gaily. Lawers House had flags hoisted from its most conspicuous points of view; and the cottages along the roadside, as well as Colonel Williamson's own residence - Tredegar Lodge - were studded with bannerettes, etc. The cottages at the Milton and Tomperran House were similarly treated. As was most meet, Comrie Railway Station floated a large banner and numerous small flags in honour of him who had done so much to place it there; and also the little church of St. Serf opposite contributed to the general display. The most prominent object on entering the village was the handsome floral arch erected on the top of the Bridge of Lednock, which bore on either side Royal crests. It formed what might be called an appropriate triumphal approach, through which the Colonel and his lady would enter the village on their way along the gaily-decorated streets to the banqueting hall.

In the evening, at six o'clock, a banquet took place in the Public Hall, where the presentations were made. The platform was beautifully decorated with flowers, etc., and presented quite an attractive appearance. For some days previous the event had been the chief topic of conversation in the village and the result was a large demand for tickets to the hall, both by ladies and gentlemen. The gallery and the side seats in the hall were reserved for the ladies, of whom there was a crowded assemblage.

To add further to the sense of great occasion, the Colonel and his wife were driven from Lawers to the Public Hall in an open carriage drawn by four spirited horses which were mounted with two red-coated postillions. A large crowd cheered enthusiastically as they went by and, on entering the hall and passing through to the platform, they received another great ovation, the menfolk cheering and waving their hats whilst the ladies waved their handkerchiefs.

Colonel Stewart of Ardvorlich presided. Several speeches were made and loyal toasts drunk before they came to the main business of the evening - the presentations.

The Testimonial read as follows:

To COLONEL D. R. WILLIAMSON OF LAWERS
Chairman of the Crieff and Comrie Railway Company

Sir,

On the successful completion of the Railway from Crieff to Comrie, a great desire has been manifested by the Inhabitants of Comrie and surrounding district that your invaluable services to the undertaking should be in some suitable way recognised by them. They confidently believe that they are indebted to your individual exertions for the accomplishment of this long cherished scheme and they especially feel that but for your untiring efforts the share capital necessary to construct the Railway could not have been raised; and, in connection with this point, they greatly appreciate the laudable example shown by you in taking up so much of the capital in your own name.

They have also seen, with admiration, your unceasing zeal in the interests of the Railway in all its stages, from the time it was first mooted till the day of its opening for traffic on 1st June 1893.

With the view to giving expression to these feelings of gratitude and admiration for your services, we, whose names are appended, formed ourselves into a Committee to receive offerings towards a Testimonial to be presented to you, and, as the result of this movement, we, on behalf of the Subscribers of the money, who number upward of 350, and among whom are many friends from a distance, have now the pleasure of presenting to you a set of 3 silver bowls, having a series of views engraved thereon, and we have also the pleasure of presenting the Hon. Mrs Williamson, your worthy partner in life, who cut the first sod of the Railway, a Silver Tea Service as a token of the respectful esteem in which she is held by all.

Along with the Address we beg to hand you a list of the names of the subscribers to the testimonial.

With the sincere wish of long life and happiness to yourself and the Honourable Mrs Williamson.

We are, sir

Your obedient Servants.

(There follows the names of the 28 members of the Committee.)

John Graham of Comrie wrote a song in honour of the occasion:

Comrie Railway Song
May we all be the better, and none be the worse,
Since not we've got hold of this grand iron horse.
May Comrie now flourish, her commerce increase;
And gentle and simple have pleasure and peace.

Chorus
Hurrah for the railway, success to it now!
We have looked for it long, and we've got it, I trow,
Hurrah for the Colonel, who worked for our good,
And our noble Directors who by him have stood.

We'll welcome the rich, we'll welcome the poor,
And those will come now who were ne'er her before.
Our mountains are grand, and our breezes are free,
And the birds they sing blithely o'er woodland and lea.

Chorus - Hurrah for our railway, etc.

Our rills are like crystal, as onward they flow;
Our Earn is calm, and its murmurs are low;
Our Lednock's a sight worth coming to see;
And our Ruchil's the emblem of all that is free.

Chorus - Hurrah for our railway, etc.

Our thanks to the Colonel, so earnest and brave,
For us and our railway, he worked like a slave.
And now from our hearts we will fervently say --
Success to us all and our useful railway.

Chorus - Hurrah for our railway, etc.

In his reply, Colonel Williamson expressed his appreciation to the Committee for honouring him in this way. He went on to praise the efforts of his fellow Directors who, he said, had given their services for no payment. Two of the company's officials, Mr Dempster (solicitor) and Mr Moncur (resident engineer) were also singled out for praise but he spoke extremely critically of the Company Secretary, Mr Shaw of Perth, with whom he had had a recent personal disagreement over the way the latter had interpreted his duties.

In conclusion the Colonel reminded his audience of the many obstacles that had been encountered along the way, particularly of the difficulty in raising sufficient capital to complete the railway, but he and his fellow Directors had persuaded a number of the merchant princes of Perth, Edinburgh and Glasgow to take shares in the company and now they had their railway.

Further toasts were proposed and drunk with enthusiasm and the village was brilliantly illuminated in the evening. But, unknown to most of the guests, this was to be the high-water mark of the long campaign to bring the railway to Comrie. Behind the scenes, things were not going well. The line's contractor, Mr Mackay, was suing for unpaid bills and, egged on by the recently-dismissed Secretary, Mr Shaw, there were discontented mutterings from shareholders who lived outside the district.

The silver bowls presented to Colonel Williamson at his Testimonial Dinner on 20th September, 1893 to celebrate the opening of the Crieff & Comrie Railway on 1st July.

Author

Chapter Six

Rumblings of Discontent

It was obvious, from a letter received by the Caledonian Railway's Finance Committee, that money was still in short supply. Early in April 1894 they received a letter from Mr Shaw enclosing a cheque for £2,000 which he asked them to accept as full payment against their bill of £2,168. Unfortunately for the new railway the Caledonian refused to reduce its bill.

Shortly afterwards Mr Shaw, who had hitherto been publicly praised for his efforts on behalf of the undertaking and for his professional competence, was dismissed by Colonel Williamson from his office as Secretary of the new company and was replaced by Mr T. Dempster, the company's solicitor.

In the light of subsequent events, it would appear that Mr Shaw had begun professionally to object to Colonel Williamson's increasing desperate attempts to keep the true financial circumstances of the undertaking from its shareholders and of his determination to resist any attempt by major shareholders from outside the district to gain representation on the Board of Directors.

In Colonel Williamson's eyes, this was personally his and Comrie's railway. He himself had contributed a large amount of money and it was only through his own efforts in travelling the country far and wide, cajoling wealthy businessmen and bankers to invest in the company, that they had raised enough money to construct the line. He was damned if he was now going to let big city businessmen interfere in the running of his company!

Mr Shaw did not take his dismissal lightly and promptly allied himself with dissident shareholders representing the 'outside' interests in Glasgow and Edinburgh. Their grievances were expressed in a letter sent to shareholders on 4th April, 1894 by Mr A. McPhail Stewart, who wrote as follows:

Dear Sir or Madam

At the last Annual Meeting of the Shareholders, a motion was submitted for the purpose of obtaining a representation on the Board of Directors from the Shareholders resident in Glasgow, Edinburgh, Dundee, and other places. The present Board of Directors (six in number) is purely local to the districts of Crieff and Comrie, while a majority of the Capital is held in other parts of the country, and mostly in the cities named. The motion, made a year ago, was only lost by two or three votes, and the Chairman then promised that the matter should be considered afresh at the next Meeting.

The successful management of our property requires good business capacity on the part of the Directors, willingness to take trouble in examining details, and association with trade and railway management in the great centres of business. In the opinion of many Shareholders, it is indispensable for the future prosperity of this Company that some new blood should be infused into the present Board. This proposal is not made in a spirit of antagonism to present Members of the Board - some of whom will, it is believed, welcome the proposal - but solely in the interest of the Company, and for the good of the property. The proposal also carries out the promises made to the Shareholders a year ago.

You are earnestly requested to sign the enclosed Form of Proxy, and send it to me by return of post.
Yours truly
    A. McPhail Stewart
On behalf of the Glasgow Committee of Shareholders.

It is true that the present Directors were all local men and some, particularly Colonel Williamson, regarded the company as their own private fiefdom. Whatever might have been promised at the previous Shareholders Meeting, he for one had no intention of letting outsiders have a say in the running of 'his' company.

News of a dispute must have circulated in the area because there was an unusually high turnout of shareholders at the next half-yearly meeting.

Mr Shaw attempted to have four dissident 'outsiders', namely Fritz Ruprecht of the North British Station Hotel (nowadays the Copthorne) in Glasgow, Major Henry Ferrie of Edinburgh, John McFarlane, writer in Glasgow, and Ebenezer Hughes of Edinburgh, legally registered as shareholders through a recent transfer of shares.

Colonel Williamson, supported by the new Secretary, Mr Dempster, refused outright to accept these persons as current shareholders on the ground that the share transfers had been received only two hours previously; too late for the Directors to have sufficient time to consider the transferees' acceptability. Mr Dempster said that the transfers would be submitted to the Directors in the ordinary course of business, (i.e. long after the meeting had ended).

A furious row erupted, with both Mr Shaw and the would-be shareholders accusing the Board of what would nowadays be termed 'gerrymandering' and accusing the Directors of illegal practices in the way they were conducting the meeting. The air was thick with accusations by the dissidents about illegal practices on the part of the Directors, which Colonel Williamson countered by sarcastically saying that their protests were being noted and the dissidents should consult their solicitors if they wished to object further.

The proxy votes asked for by Mr Stewart in his letter to shareholders were the next item on the agenda. Colonel Williamson said that these had been counted; 1,221 proxies were in favour of re-electing the present Board and only 426 were in favour of introducing new blood.

Mr Shaw refused to accept the figures and demanded that the proxies should be handed to him for examination. This was refused but he was allowed to go to the counting table to examine the proxies himself. In the end, he and his supporters had to accept the Chairman's figures and so the meeting got under way again.

The accounts for the previous half-year ended 31st January, 1893 were then presented to the meeting and Mr Shaw immediately launched into a bitter and detailed criticism of them. He began by accusing the Directors of suppressing certain proxy votes he had received and went on to say that the Directors' estimate of a further total of £3,300 capital expenditure was absolutely inaccurate and the true figure should be more like £6,000-£9,000. The Chairman countered this by pointing out that the estimate of £3,300 was for the next half-year, not the total remaining cost.

In Mr Shaw's opinion, the whole accounts were 'studded with the grossest illegalities and irregularities and should be remitted back to the Directors for revision and brought before another meeting' (by that time, of course, his allies would have become shareholders).

Arrears on calls had been reduced from £259 to £175, the overdraft of £6,286 to the bank had been extinguished and replaced by around £2,800 in the bank.

Instead of paying interest at 5½ per cent on the overdraft they were now paying 3½ per cent on the mortgages.

At this point the Chairman moved, and another Director, Sir Robert Moncrieffe seconded, the adoption of the report and accounts. Mr Stewart, the dissenting merchant of Glasgow, moved that the report and accounts should not be adopted, 'being in many respects illegal and incorrect, and that they be remitted back to the directors for amendment in compliance with the Acts of Parliament'. They also wished to know under what Act of Parliament they were being excluded from being registered and being allowed to vote.

Mr Shaw pointed out that the accounts showed uncalled capital of £1,446 which he considered showed gross negligence on the part of the Board in allowing money to lie in some shareholders' pockets whilst the company was paying interest on bank overdrafts, etc. He also asked what was the company's indebtedness to the Caledonian Railway Company, its law agents and other parties, which he maintained would account for far more than the estimated £3,300. Furthermore, the contractor (Mackay) was claiming over £6,000 as still being due to him and which was likely to end in serious litigation, against which not a penny had been provided.

The discussion became very heated when Colonel Williamson refused to disclose how much money the Company owed at the date of the accounts (31st January) or the extent of claims against it. In his view, they owed the contractors nothing.

In spite of the rebels' opposition, the report and accounts were adopted and Colonel Williamson and his fellow-Directors were re-elected.

It appears that the mood of the majority of the shareholders who attended the meeting was in favour of maintaining the status quo, and most of the newspaper reports of the proceedings were complimentary towards Colonel Williamson and highly critical of the rebels. However, the latter did have some support, as evidenced by the following comment in a local newspaper:

If the Comrie Railway does not promise to be a paying concern, to all appearances, judging from the last meeting of the shareholders, the company's meetings promise to be lively. We are not of those who have been enamoured with the businesslike way this railway undertaking has been carried out. With the fact that there were no serious engineering difficulties in its construction, and that nearly one half of the distance between Crieff and Comrie was almost as level as a bowling green, yet that it should cost so much money for its construction one way and another, shows that there is a screw loose somewhere. We are therefore not surprised that shareholders - particularly those at a distance - should feel somewhat annoyed at the way the railway has been managed, and that there should be a desire for a change in the Directorate. We take it for granted that a very considerable amount of the capital for the construction of the line was subscribed in Edinburgh, Glasgow and elsewhere out of the district, and we do not see either the justice or the wisdom of choosing all the Directors from this particular locality. Depend upon it, such a dog-in-the-manger kind of policy may lead in the long run to 'firing out' one of the Directors, and it may be the Chairman himself. That gentleman's performance at the meeting referred to was hardly what might be called a success. There was too much sarcasm that was not clever, and too little conciliation shown. From what we have heard we very much question if the accounts submitted to the shareholders show all the claims due by the Company. We would not be astonished

Largest Shareholders in Dundee) ~~ARM~~
" Edin } *adverse full strength* — 474 ~~less~~ 48
" Glasgow) *Favourable strength* — 1205
                            6
                    121 +10 = 12
Late +ddd
          Proxy   Total − 131

Crieff and Comrie Railway Co.

~~FCR~~   *433 Votes of Holders of limited amount*
                                     Total   132

Salary of Directors —

DEAR SIR OR MADAM,

    At the last Annual Meeting of the Shareholders, a motion was submitted for the purpose of obtaining a representation on the Board of Directors from the Shareholders resident in Glasgow, Edinburgh, Dundee, and other places. The present Board of Directors (six in number) is purely local to the districts of Crieff and Comrie, while a majority of the Capital is held in other parts of the country, and mostly in the cities named. The motion, made a year ago, was only lost by two or three *[3 4 25]* votes, and the Chairman then promised that the matter should be considered afresh at the next Meeting.

    The successful management of our property requires good business capacity on the part of *Salary £?* the Directors, willingness to take trouble in examining details, and association with trade and *Shaw. Dey* railway management in the great centres of business. In the opinion of many Shareholders, it is *£75 £25* indispensable for the future prosperity of this Company that some new blood should be infused into the present Board. This proposal is not made in a spirit of antagonism to present Members *Office* of the Board—some of whom will, it is believed, welcome the proposal,—but solely in the interest *Slaym Coun* of the Company, and for the good of the property. The proposal also carries out the promises *£21 £5* made to the Shareholders a year ago.

    You are earnestly requested to sign the enclosed Form of Proxy, and send it to me by return of post.

Who is Mr Shaw? Management other Coys
False Proxys before of noon

      Yours truly,   *secretion of our Knk —*

               A. McP. STEWART.

On behalf of the Glasgow Committee of Shareholders.

Want of Business Capacity hand
in false Proxys

48 OSWALD STREET,   *Who is Mr Shaw?*
GLASGOW, 4th April, 1894.   " " Mr McStewart, Merchant?

What is at the Bottom of this ~~Fast~~ Circular?   *Two Shares = £10 — paid on 7 April*
The Bills stuck up at Night   *Langlands p & G, Chyae on 9th Apl*
The ½d Stamps

in the long run to hear that all or nearly all the money the Company is empowered to borrow will be needed. As it is, the fact that nearly £55,000 has been expended to make a line of railway not six miles in length, is pretty good evidence that 'fresh blood' would not be a bad thing in the Directorate, and if more evidence were needed, the 'lofty' reply of the Chairman to Mr Stewart as to the selection of Directors supplies it.

The next half-yearly meeting, held in the David and Selina Hall in October 1894, was again well-attended but was a much quieter affair that the last one. The dissident shareholders appear to have given up their fight for representation on the Board but, following Sir Robert Moncreiffe's recent retirement due to ill-health, the vacancy had been filled by Mr James G. Orchar, a businessman from Broughty Ferry, so the company gained new blood on the Board after all.

The Chairman reported that the railway was in a prosperous state and that a dividend of 1½ per cent free of income tax was being declared for the half-year. He thought it was most unusual for a new railway to be able to declare any dividend at all in only its second half-year of operation and he fully believed that this rate of dividend would be maintained or even bettered in their next half-year.

Ex-Provost MacRosty of Crieff, in seconding the adoption of the accounts, remarked that anyone driving through the village nowadays found some stir and bustle. Summer visitors were arriving by the hundred, flocking all over the place, spending their money and otherwise improving the position of the community.

The accounts showed that £44,703 of the £45,000 authorised capital had been taken up and £10,000 of the £15,000 authorised loans on mortgages. They had spent £9,279 on purchasing land, £36,397 on constructing the line and station, £2,084 on engineering expenses, £2,076 on legal expenses, £1,289 on Parliamentary expenses and £2,508 on other expenses, making a total capital expenditure of £53,633 with a probable further £1,000 still to come.

Revenue in the six months to 31st July had been as follows:

Passengers	637
Goods	332
Parcels	87
Minerals	68
Mails	35
Livestock	24
Other	14
Total	£1,197

Out of this, £591 had been paid to the Caledonian for working the line and other expenses such as rent, rates and administration had amounted to £193, leaving a surplus of £413. Passenger train mileage had been 10,806 and goods mileage had been 2,526 miles.

By now the line was attracting a fair amount of tourist traffic. In May the *Dundee Courier* reported that this summer would set a new record for railway excursion facilities in the area and cited a new series of afternoon trips laid on by the Caledonian from Dundee to Almondbank, Crieff and Comrie, the fares being 1s. 3d., 2s. and 2s. 6d. respectively.

Visitors to Comrie in June included 500 employees of James Keiller's confectionery works at Dundee who arrived for the day in a specially chartered train.

At the next half-yearly meeting, held in April 1895, the Chairman reported that the revenue had increased significantly over the corresponding half-year in 1893, i.e. the first six months of operation. The operating surplus had increased to £624 and the Directors were recommending another payment of 1½ per cent to shareholders net of income tax. He referred to the fact that all the great railway companies in Scotland had had a very difficult half-year whereas their little company had increased its revenue in every department.

He went on to point out that in 1859 the Crieff Junction Railway's total revenue had been £2,605 which was similar to what their own line was now achieving. Thirty years later, in 1889, the Crieff Junction's revenue had increased to £24,928 and he did not see any reason why their own line could not look forward to similar prosperity. He hoped the day was not too far distant when the shareholders would receive payment in full for what they had paid out in the purchase of their shares, and he did not think that anyone would lose a farthing by the shares they had taken in the railway.

No mention was made of the claim hanging over the company from the contractors, Mackay & Son, in respect of unpaid accounts. They were claiming a sum of £11,150 from the company including £5,900 as the balance due for the work they had done and £5,000 for alleged breach of contract.

Mackay & Son v. The Crieff & Comrie Railway

It had been agreed at the start of the contract that the Engineer of the line, Mr Young, should act as arbitrator in cases of dispute between the company and themselves. Mackay & Son now claimed that Mr Young had acted improperly and fraudulently because he was also a shareholder in the company and could not, therefore, make an impartial judgement. Furthermore, he had had meetings with the Chairman and written letters to two other Directors in terms that suggested that he had pre-judged the question of how much was owed to the contractors.

The company countered by saying that Mr Young had always said that he would not deal with any questions which were not by the contract left to his sole discretion. They also counter-claimed for liquidated damages caused by the contractors' failure to complete the line within the stipulated period, and also sums paid to third parties as damages.

The case of Mackay & Son v. Crieff & Comrie Railway and John Young, C.E. came before Lord Low in the Court of Session in October 1895 and makes interesting reading.

The contract for constructing the line had been agreed at £21,055 with a further £200 for maintaining the line for 12 months after the line had been opened to the public. Payments would be made to the contractors at the rate of 90 per cent of the work completed according to the Engineer's (Mr Young) certificate and were payable one month after the date of the certificate. When the line had been completed the total amount of construction work would be re-measured and the balance paid to the contractors within three months, less a reasonable retention determined by the Engineer. The contract bound the contractors to complete the works within 17 months of being given possession of the ground.

Because the railway company was always chronically short of money to meet its commitments, the contractors were asked at the outset if they would take shares on account of the contract price. This they declined to do in principle but said that, if the contract price was increased by £750, they would take shares to a value of £1,805 against the contract. The railway company agreed to this and the contract price was increased to £21,805.

Protracted negotiations with the Crieff Town Council and Thomas Graham Stirling delayed the start of the project and the contractor complained bitterly that, in consequence, he was only able to work on disjointed sections of the line instead of being given possession of the whole length. This was especially inefficient where the line passed through the Strowan estate and included the 90 yds-long tunnel, because the amount of spoil dug on the Crieff side of the tunnel was almost the same as the quantity needed to build the long embankment on the Comrie side. Unfortunately, this spoil could not be moved and the embankment built until the tunnel had been driven through the hill, and this was delayed for many months whilst arbitration took place over the compensation payable to Mr Graham Stirling.

Moreover, they claimed that the Engineer was forever making changes to the specification.

Similar delays occurred at the Crieff end of the line where the cost of the engineering works accounted for around a third of the total cost of the contract. The contractors claimed that the railway company were at fault in not giving them possession early enough so that they could establish a service line to the Caledonian's rails and so expedite their own construction work.

They also claimed that the railway company, instead of channelling amendments through themselves, had sometimes directly instructed sub-contractors to alter the heights of various bridges and change the levels along the line. This had incurred considerable additional expense in additional embanking and ballasting. On other occasions their workmen had been idle because materials promised to be delivered to a certain point on the line on a certain date had failed to materialise. They claimed that, on some occasions, the material had not even been ordered by the promised delivery date (this was obviously because the company didn't have the money to pay for the materials!).

Even worse, they cited an occasion when they arrived at Comrie station to lay the sidings and found the ground already occupied by workmen who were laying cheap second-hand rails for the sidings. These workmen had been employed directly by the railway company and immediately took possession of the materials brought along by the contractors' workmen, leaving the latter standing around idle! Furthermore, their workmen had been prevented from carrying out contracted work at Crieff and Comrie because the railway company had themselves sub-contracted the work to another contractor who had, only shortly before, resigned as a Director of the company.

They further claimed that Mr Young's certificates had consistently understated the amount of work they had completed and, even then, they had had to wait an unreasonable amount of time for payment. When they had attempted to appoint their own valuer to liaise with Mr Young on the valuations, he had not co-operated in the slightest.

The railway had opened for traffic on 1st June, 1893 but the contractors claimed they had not been paid the balance of the money due to them, amounting to £5,951 and that the railway company was endeavouring to avoid payment. They also claimed a further £5,000 damages for alleged breach of contract.

In reply, the railway company claimed that they had given the contractor possession of the whole of the line within a reasonable time and that subsequent delays were entirely due to the contractor's dilatory and unskilful workmanship. In the circumstances they not only had the contractual right to directly engage their own workmen in order to minimize delays but they also had the right to charge the contractors £10 for each of the 423 days the contract was late, plus a further £109 to people whose property they had damaged.

The railway company denied all the contractors' claims against them and asked that their claims should be rejected. In truth, the situation bears all the hallmarks of a chronic shortage of money on their part, the amount of capital raised always lagging behind their commitments, and of Colonel Williamson personally intervening to push on with the work regardless of the terms of the contract. They denied virtually the whole of the contractors' claims and submitted that they owed the contractors nothing.

Lord Low's judgement was that Mr Young, by his actions and the letters he had written to various members of the Board, had disqualified himself from acting as arbiter in regard to the balance claimed by Mackay & Son. However, he found no evidence to substantiate the accusations of fraud and, because he regarded these accusations as having been made recklessly against a body of Directors and a professional gentleman, he refused to grant Mackay & Son their costs, even though they had won this part of their lawsuit.

But that was not the end of the matter. He allowed Mackay & Son time to furnish proof of certain of their allegations and the claim had still not been settled two years later when far more serious problems overtook the railway company.

Chapter Seven

The Last Years of Independence

The next half-yearly meeting was held in the David and Selina Hall in October 1895. The Chairman reported that revenue had again increased significantly compared with the previous half-year and, moreover, their office expenses had decreased. In spite of one or two hints that they could have increased the dividend, it was being maintained at 1½ per cent. The adoption of the report and accounts was seconded by ex-Provost MacRostie of Crieff who complimented the Directors on their prudence in building up a nest-egg that could be used for the extension of the railway to join up with the Callander & Oban trunk line in the north - probably at Glenoglehead.

This was a very interesting comment because it shows that the original intention of extending the line was for it to turn north-west just short of Lochearnhead village and run parallel to the Callander & Oban on the opposite slopes of Glen Ogle to meet the trunk line near Killin Junction. This is borne out by an undated sketch map of the Crieff & Comrie Railway drawn by John Young, which subsequently accompanied the Bill of the new railway when it was placed before Parliament in 1897.

During the last few months yet another petition had been sent to the Caledonian by the inhabitants of Monzievaird and Strowan, asking them to institute a station and siding at Thornhill, but their request had again been declined. Was there a genuine need for a station to serve the needs of the district or was this a final attempt by Thomas Graham Stirling, in the last year of his long life, marshalling his tenants to get his new bridge and road diversion? We shall never know.

On the other hand, the Caley did agree to put in a siding and grant a lease of ground at Comrie for Hugh Morgan to set up a sawmill.

The next half-yearly meeting was held in the David and Selina Hall in April 1896. The Chairman reported that revenue had increased by around 7 per cent compared with the corresponding period in 1895 and that the dividend would be maintained at 1½ per cent. In all other respects there had been little change.

Mr Carolus Home Graham Stirling (old Thomas Graham Stirling's son and heir) was at the meeting and asked whether the company would put in a siding at Monzievaird. He pointed out that last year a petition, signed by all the inhabitants and offering a contribution of £100, had been presented to the Directors and he was now, on behalf of his father, offering a further £100 towards its construction.

Colonel Williamson gave Carolus a non-committal reply, assuring him that they wished to help the people who lived in the parish of Monzievaird but pointing out that the cost of constructing a siding would probably wipe out the shareholders' dividend for the next 12 months. However, he and the other Directors would see what they could do to accommodate their request if it was for the good of the company.

In truth, the Directors probably felt that this was yet another attempt by the Laird of Strowan to get the old bridge moved and rebuilt at the company's expense. However, later that year, the old man died at the age of 85 and nothing further seems to have been heard of the proposal.

The only notable accident on the line appears to have happened on 8th August, 1896 when the 11.23 am passenger train from Crieff Junction (Gleneagles) hit the buffer beam at Comrie station. The beam was demolished and the earth bank behind it was pushed back; the leading wheels of the engine were derailed and 15 passengers were injured.

The driver reported that he had shut off steam as usual when approaching the station but his Westinghouse brake had failed to work and the train had continued at its normal speed until it hit the buffers. It does not appear that the guard had appreciated the situation and he did not attempt to apply his own brake.

The engine driver, Mungo Headrick, the fireman, Alexander Ogston, the guard, Peter Taylor, and the Crieff station porter, James Parkinson, were all suspended from duty and were subsequently dismissed. The Directors received petitions and letters from the public asking for clemency on behalf of the driver and guard but decided to take no further action. Subsequently the driver and guard were awarded one-off payments of £35 each and that appears to have been the end of the matter.

The next half-yearly meeting of shareholders was held in October 1896 when the Chairman reported another increase in revenue and profits. This time the revenue had increased only slightly but expenditure had been reduced. The shares were now trading on the Glasgow Stock Exchange at 80s., their highest level yet.

The dividend was maintained at 1½ per cent. The Chairman said that the Directors had considered increasing it to 2 per cent but had chosen to increase their capital reserves instead. However, he had no doubt that they would see 2 per cent in the next half-year.

He also indicated that the company was considering whether their line should now be extended westwards to Lochearnhead. His personal opinion was that such an extension would immediately double their revenue but at this stage he was not prepared to comment further.

A half-yearly meeting of the shareholders was held in the David and Selina Hall in October 1897. Compared to meetings in earlier years this was very low-key, the only attendees being Colonel Williamson, four fellow-Directors and four shareholders.

Colonel Williamson reported that the railway's financial situation was not quite so satisfactory as those in past half-years, but he still thought they might look forward to greater prosperity in the future. All the same, the Directors again declared a dividend of 1½ per cent on Ordinary Share Capital.

The Meeting lasted less than five minutes. At its conclusion the Chairman said that an important meeting of Directors must now be held. The purpose of this meeting was none other than to discuss selling their company to the mighty Caledonian Railway. The logic behind this move was twofold.

Firstly, the Directors had realised that the line would never pay the level of dividend to shareholders that had been anticipated in the heady days of 1890 when they had persuaded lots of individuals to invest in the new company. Moreover, the country now appeared to moving into a period of economic recession; the last half-year's trading had been at a lower level than previously and, further, they thought the next year would be even worse.

Secondly, Mackay & Son's claim against them was still not settled in the courts of law. The Directors realised that the eventual outcome might leave the company without sufficient money to settle the contractors' claim which might amount to as much as £5,000, a very significant sum in those days.

Negotiations were commenced with the Caledonian and a Special Meeting of the Crieff & Comrie Railway shareholders was held on 9th February, 1898, when the motion was put to them that they should accept the Caledonian's offer.

By this time the Caledonian Railway was casting its eyes westwards along Strathearn. It already operated the trains on the smaller railways that ran from Stirling and Perth as far as Comrie and it had invested heavily in the new railway company that was now being built to connect Comrie with the Callander & Oban line near Lochearnhead. This would give them control over much of the traffic passing between the West Highlands and Eastern Scotland.

In common with most Victorian railway companies, the Caledonian's motives were partly expansionist and partly protectionist. It wanted above all to keep its deadly rival, the North British Railway, out of what it saw as a potentially lucrative direct East-West trade.

Because of this, its terms for buying the Crieff & Comrie Railway were generous. It proposed to repay shareholders their capital investment of £45,000 in full. Moreover, it would take over the company's £10,000 mortgages and also settle Mackay & Son's claim for damages, which were eventually settled for the sum of £5,000.

As always, Colonel Williamson chaired the meeting of the Crieff & Comrie Railway shareholders. Whilst he must have been bitterly disappointed that the railway he had fought so hard to bring to Comrie was now going to pass out of local control, he was able to point out to shareholders that they had been repaid their investment in full as well as having received a small dividend during the line's short independent existence.

He recommended shareholders to accept the Caledonian's offer, pointing out that whilst the Caledonian's present board of Directors was favourably disposed towards them, future Directors might not take the same attitude and might starve their little line of traffic or, even worse, might even refuse to work it.

His mixture of practicality and sentimentality worked, particularly with local shareholders who, in many cases, had invested their savings out of patriotism for their locality rather than in the hope of achieving wealth. Even the outside shareholders appeared satisfied with the outcome.

The Caledonian absorbed the railway on 1st August, 1898 by virtue of an Act of Parliament. So ended the independent life of the Crieff & Comrie Railway. It had benefited the village and local shareholders had not lost their investments.

The railway now settled down to a quiet existence and resisted another attempt in 1898, this time by Sir Keith Murray of Ochtertyre, to have a station built at Thornhill.

But Colonel Williamson had not finished with local railways . . .

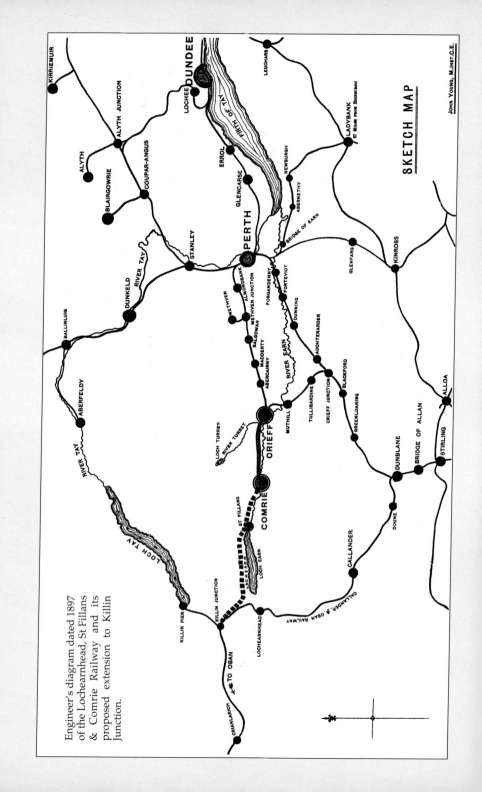

Engineer's diagram dated 1897 of the Lochearnhead, St Fillans & Comrie Railway and its proposed extension to Killin Junction.

SKETCH MAP

JOHN YOUNG, M.INST.C.E.

Chapter Eight

The Lochearnhead, St Fillans & Comrie Railway

It had long been the Caledonian Railway's ambition to make an east-to-west railway connection through Strathearn. As we have already seen the Scottish Central Railway had reached Stirling, Dunblane and Perth from the South in 1848. On 1st July, 1858 a new line, the Dunblane, Doune & Callander Railway was opened. It was a short line of only 11 miles; it took only two years to build and was worked by the Scottish Central from the beginning.

This was in complete contrast to its extension, the Callander & Oban Railway Company, which was authorised in 1865 to carry the railway onwards through the mountains of Perthshire and Argyllshire to Oban. Serious financial difficulties delayed the completion of the line and it was not until 1880 that it was opened throughout. It was worked by the Caledonian Railway from its opening but maintained its nominal independence until the Grouping of 1923.

Railways had reached Crieff from Crieff Junction (the present day Gleneagles) in 1856, from Perth via Methven in 1867 and were extended to Comrie in 1893. This left a gap of some 15 miles through upper Strathearn to the nearest point on the Callander & Oban line near Lochearnhead.

A year before the Crieff & Comrie Railway was absorbed by the Caledonian in 1898, there had been moves to promote a railway that would connect these two points. This was achieved by the passing of the Lochearnhead, St Fillans & Comrie Railway Company Railway Act on 6th August, 1897 which, unusually, was passed unopposed through both Houses of Parliament.

Perhaps in anticipation of the environmental lobby of a century later, an MP proposed that a Select Committee should be appointed to consider the railway in the context of the environment. This was unprecedented at the time and a committee was formed which gave the railway a 'clean bill of health' and the Royal Assent was received on 6th August, 1897.

All the same the Chairman, Col Home-Drummond, took special steps to ensure that the railway did not obtrude on the landscape. For instance, at Tynreoch (near St Fillans) the railway was laid for some distance along the foot of a rocky slope with the road running alongside. In the same area the company moved the public road back 22 yards and laid down a plantation so that the railway would be hidden from road travellers. Newspaper comments towards this landscaping were favourable and it was said that, in a few years time, the railway would be hidden from the public view after leaving Comrie until within a mile of St Fillans, where it was so high above the road as to be invisible.

The authorised capital of the company was £165,000 comprised of 16,500 shares of £10 each. The Caledonian Railway subscribed half the capital (£82,500) on condition that it had the option within five years of the opening of the railway to take over the whole undertaking. The Directors of the new company were:

Colonel H.E.S. Home-Drummond of Blair-Drummond, J.P., D.L. and Convenor of the
County Council of Perthshire (Chairman)
John A. Dewar, Esq, Lord Provost of the City of Perth, Balcraig, Perth
John M. Fraser, Esq. of Invermay, Rosemount, Perth (Managing Director of Messrs
Macdonald, Fraser & Co. Ltd)
J. Badenach Nicholson, Esq. of Glenbervie, Fordoun (Director of the Town & County
Bank Ltd and of the Caledonian Railway Company)
Colonel D.R. Williamson of Lawers, J.P. and D.L. of Perthshire.

Apart from Colonel Williamson the only link with the Crieff & Comrie
Company was the employment of Thomas Dempster as Secretary.

This time there was no question of the new company's Directors being drawn
purely from local worthies. Too much outside capital had been invested. Their
bankers were the Bank of Scotland, the Royal Bank of Scotland and the Town &
County Bank, they employed brokers in both Edinburgh and Glasgow and their
engineers were an eminent firm from Glasgow, Messrs Crouch & Hogg.

Its Prospectus, which was not issued until February 1899, announced that the
company had been incorporated for the purpose of constructing a railway about
15 miles in length from Comrie to Lochearnhead. In addition to serving the
district through which it would pass, its construction would connect the line
from Dundee, Perth and Crieff with the Callander and Oban line and thus
complete the link required to form a through route between the East Coast
Counties and the West Highlands.

The Prospectus went on to state that:

The traffic on the line would consist of livestock, large numbers of which were sent
from the West and Central Highlands to the Perth Sales and for wintering in Eastern
Counties, agricultural produce, timber and general merchandise, A very large summer
and tourist traffic existed, at present accommodated by coaches, and this would be very
greatly increased because of the increased facilities. The railway would pass through
some of the most beautiful scenery in Scotland and the finest views in the district would
be seen by travelling over it. Both at St Fillans and Lochearnhead there is excellent
feuing ground available for the erection of summer residences, in addition to those
already built, and as the proposed line will afford a direct railway route either via
Callander or via Crieff from Edinburgh and Glasgow, and will also bring Dundee and
Perth within an easy distance of the Comrie and Lochearnside districts, a large number
of summer residents will, as is usual in similar cases, find their way into them.

It is, however, from its importance as a through route that the Railway may be
expected to derive its principal traffic and to be of the greatest benefit to the country. The
opening up of the Western Highlands has in the past been carried out chiefly in
connection with the west and south, but the proposed line will complete a direct railway
route from the East to the West Coasts through Central Scotland. It will thus be seen that
a large traffic may be anticipated over the proposed railway between the East Coast
Ports and Coal Fields on the one hand and the West Highlands on the other.

The proposed railway is more favourably situated than such railways as the Callander
and Oban and the Crieff and Comrie, inasmuch as it will, immediately on its opening,
obtain the benefit of the traffic already existing on these railways, a large portion of
which will from the first pass over it, and it is certain that traffic will rapidly be further
developed by its construction.

The published accounts of the Callander and Oban Railway show that the present
revenue of that line is at the rate of £796 per mile per annum. Such a revenue on the

proposed railway would yield a dividend on the estimated cost of nearly 4% per annum. As the railway will connect the Callander and Oban with the Northern and Central Sections of the Caledonian Railway, there is no reason to expect that a less revenue will be earned on it than on the Callander and Oban; even, however, if the revenue earned were considerably smaller, it would still yield a satisfactory dividend.

The estimated cost of the Railway is £160,000, and it is intended to commence its construction as soon as the Contracts can be let.

The Caledonian Railway had agreed to work, manage and maintain the line in return for 50 per cent of the gross receipts. By an Agreement made in October 1898 they not only subscribed half of the issued capital but also promised that if they exercised their option to purchase the line within five years of its being opened for traffic, they would pay par value for the portion of the Share Capital held by other shareholders.

Tenders were immediately invited for the construction of the line in two sections: Contract No. 1 was for the 5.75 miles from Comrie to St Fillans and this would be followed later by Contract No. 2 for the remaining 9.5 miles to Balquhidder.

Very little enthusiasm was shown by the railway contracting fraternity. Only one tender was received for Contract No 1; this was from John Paton, C.E. of Glasgow. When a re-advertisement failed to bring any further responses, his tender of £78,130 13s. 1d. was accepted in May 1899 and he took up residence at 29 Dundas Street, Comrie.

At first it was not intended to have a formal ceremony to mark the cutting of the first turf but, in the end, hasty arrangements were made for a low-key ceremony on 12th June, 1899. This was carried out by Colonel Williamson in the Laggan Park adjoining Comrie station. Although he was not the Chairman of the new railway, he had been one of its chief promoters and the extension from Comrie began on his estate.

He spoke of the advantages that the new railway would bring by opening up through communication between East and West, and it would be the means of circulating between £70,000 and £80,000 in the district within the next four years.

After the Revd W. Hall of the United Presbyterian Church had offered up prayers for the success of the undertaking and the safety and comfort of the workmen employed on it, the spectators enjoyed refreshments. Afterwards, Colonel Williamson provided a free table at several of the hotels in the village and many villagers spent the evening dancing in a large wooden building that had been erected at the station.

The plan of the line placed before Parliament shows it starting level under the road at the west end of Comrie station and then climbing steadily on an embankment behind the village on a gradient of 1 in 70 as far as Dundas Street which it crossed by a bridge of 33 feet span and 16 feet high. From here it went onto a masonry viaduct 93 feet long across the River Earn.

In order to cross the railway line adjacent to the station, the public road had to be raised 9 ft 6 in. above its existing level on an approach gradient of 1 in 30. A plan of the layout of Comrie station shows that the sidings were extended and now included stables.

**LOCHEARNHEAD HOTEL,
PERTHSHIRE. N.B.**

E. MAISEY, PROPRIETOR

May 19th 1899

Col: Williamson

Dear Sir. I have to thank
you for your telegram
of date informing me that
the Railway Contract to
St Fillans is settled, and in
start to be made at once.
That it has reached this
stage at last, after many
battles through evil report
and good report, we are,
I think indebted to you.
and that for your unwearying
energy, it is said no doubt
have fallen through at

least for a considerable
period.

But I will itself meet
have reluctantly brought
about its accomplishment.
In my own name
and in name of the Committee
here, I beg to thank you.
and to express I so hope
that you will come, be
spared to see the trains
teeming through from
Comrie to Lochearnhead.

I remain,
Dear Sir,

Yours most obt

E. Maisey

Chairman of
Lochearnhead Committee

A congratulatory letter to Colonel Williamson from the Chairman of the committee formed at Lochearnhead to promote the extension of the railway westwards from Comrie. It refers to the contract for the first section, from Comrie to St Fillans, having been let.

The embankment cut across Mill Lane (nowadays Nurse's Lane) which not only served the now-closed sawmill and meal mill but also gave access to Comrie House. This problem was overcome by constructing a new service road which ran parallel to the railway from the Comrie House driveway to a new exit onto the Crieff Road. This meant that there were three almost identical bridges crossing the Lednock within a few yards of each other: the service road, the railway and the Crieff road.

A footbridge over the railway was erected in Mill Lane, similar to the one that connected the two platforms at the station.

As major shareholders on the new line the Caledonian's Board of Directors met regularly to review its progress and to authorise progress payments to its contractor. A meeting of the Directors of the new railway held on 27th November, 1899 (Colonel Williamson was absent through illness) was told that Lord Ancaster had refused to accept £4,000 exclusive of his tenants' claims for severance, etc. It was agreed that a Statutory Notice for possession of the ground should be served on his Lordship and the matter should fall into arbitration.

A letter had been received from Captain Carolus Graham Stirling who was concerned about possible flooding near the Mill of Ross and the damage that might be caused. Crouch & Hogg had replied that the construction of the railway would have no such injurious effect but if any protective works were to be put up the best way would be a concrete wall.

But their biggest problem at that time was one of their own making - one which occupied the newspapers for months and became known as 'The affair of the Colonel and the Lednock Bridge'.

The old stone bridge over the Lednock had been built in 1799. It was a substantial structure with three arches but was only 15 feet wide and was set at an angle to the approach roads on either side. Moreover, it had steep gradients on either side of its crown; a local newspaper correspondent commented that cyclists knew to make a spurt up one side and thank their fortune if, when they reached the crest, they were not pitched headlong among the 16 legs of the four-horse St Fillans coach!

Caledonian Railway's connecting road coach (Lochearnhead area?)   *J. Macintosh*

In September 1894 a public meeting, chaired by Colonel Williamson, had been held in the David and Selina Hall to gain support for lobbying the Perthshire County Council as regards rebuilding the bridge, but they were unsuccessful.

Now, in 1899 and as part of their negotiations with the Central District Committee of Perthshire County Council concerning how the new line would cross various roads on its route, the railway company offered to replace the old bridge over the Lednock with a modern 25 ft-wide bowstring bridge which would be both straight and level. They were not compelled to rebuild this bridge in addition to providing a necessary road bridge over their railway line a few yards further on but they obviously felt that this would smooth their negotiations with the Council.

The Council were so delighted with this offer that they offered to contribute £300 towards the cost of the bridge if the approaches were also improved. The railway company's engineers drew up a plan, which was approved by the Council's Engineer, for the new bridge and its approaches to continue the straight line of Drummond Street eastwards to where it could join the already-straight Crieff road. Unfortunately, the planners had neglected to consult Colonel Williamson before they came to their agreement.

The Colonel had once been a staunch Presbyterian, attending the White Church in Comrie, but he had subsequently transferred his allegiance to the Episcopalian doctrine. In 1884 he had built St Serf's Episcopalian Church on a piece of his land adjoining the Laggan Park, in a sylvan setting close to the river and screened from the passing traffic by a line of mature lime trees.

The planned layout of the new bridge and its approaches meant acquiring a small section of land owned by Colonel Williamson in front of St Serf's and cutting down the lime trees which screened it from the main road.

When he was shown the plans he almost exploded with rage! The engineers were sent off with the proverbial fleas in their ears and told to come back with a revised plan that would preserve the line of trees. This they did but the result was a bend in the approach roads on both sides of the bridge.

Colonel Williamson was happy with the new layout and agreed the revised plan personally with the Caledonian Railway's General Manager, Sir James Thompson. In a letter to the Colonel dated 10th January, 1900 Mr W. Patrick, their Assistant General Manager, said he thought it necessary that a plan should be signed along with the agreement. He suggested that Colonel Williamson should sign it on condition that he obtained an undertaking from the Lochearnhead company agreeing that the plan of road as arranged between himself and Sir James Thompson dated 11th August, 1899 be adhered to, and that the Lochearnhead company should only be entitled to take the portion of ground and trees in front of the Episcopalian Church in the event of its being ultimately compelled under the Agreement with the District Committee to make the road and bridge over the Lednock, as claimed by the District Committee.

Sir James Thompson approved of this way of arranging the matter and offered to send Colonel Williamson a draft of the undertaking which the Lochearnhead company would require to give him.

The Directors, for their part, resolved to send a letter to the District Council saying that the construction of the road bridge would be in accordance with the plan prepared by Messrs Crouch & Hogg and dated 11th August, 1899 and that it was only on the understanding that this plan should be adopted that the arrangements were made with Colonel Williamson for the acquisition of the necessary ground.

It was now the turn of the District Council to explode with rage. They insisted that they had already come to a legally-binding agreement with the railway company that the road and bridge would run in a straight line from Drummond Street. They did not want to perpetuate any bends in the road! Unfortunately for them, the legal agreement had made no reference to exactly how the approach roads should be laid out.

The railway company, not wishing to offend the Colonel, pointed out to the District Council that the proposed approach road from Drummond Street would now be much wider at 34 feet whilst the road on the other side of the bridge would be no less than 56 feet wide and be in line with the station approach, making it safer for rail travellers because a footpath would be built along that side of the bridge.

In March a meeting held between the two sides ended acrimoniously. Mr John Carmichael, who attended on behalf of Comrie Parish Council, reported back to his Council that, 'he was not going to state what remarks were made on the occasion but he felt, after what had been said, that there was little hope of an amicable settlement'.

Colonel Williamson absolutely refused to grant any ground opposite the church or remove any of the trees there. For their part the District Council not only refused to accept Colonel Williamson's proposed diversion but also threatened to withdraw their offer of a £300 contribution towards the cost of the new bridge and sue for damages.

'In that case', said the Railway Directors, 'we will not build you a new road bridge at all'.

A few days later the Comrie Parish Council met and decided to send a deputation comprising Messrs John Carmichael, John Graham and James Comrie to Colonel Williamson, to ask him the extent of the land he would be prepared to give for road widening. The Colonel received them cordially and they all went to the locality of the bridge where the Colonel said that he would give, free of charge, sufficient land to the north and east of the present bridge as would allow the road to be made as straight as possible so long as the trees were preserved.

The District Council was still not satisfied and they huffed and puffed for several more weeks. Eventually, after months of acrimony, they reluctantly agreed at their meeting held on 9th July, 1900 to accept Colonel Williamson's plan as there was no possibility of obtaining the ground from him for the original agreed plan.

So ended the Battle of the Lednock Bridge. As usual Colonel Williamson had emerged victorious from a skirmish against overwhelming odds and its legacy remains, in the bends in the road on either side of the river and the former railway overbridge on the A85 at the east end of Drummond Street.

And the lime trees are still standing proudly in front of St Serf's church to this day!

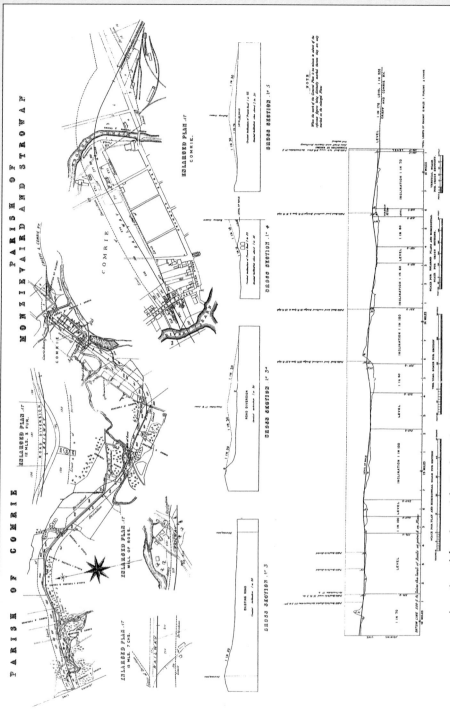

A section of the plans of the Lochearnhead, St Fillans & Comrie Railway laid before Parliament in 1897.

Chapter Nine

Extension to Balquhidder

After the first turf was cut on 12th June, 1899 work began in earnest on the extension westwards from Comrie to St Fillans. Around 400 navvies and some 30 horses were set to work on various parts of the line.

The plant for constructing the new railway began arriving at Comrie station in June 1899 and the *Strathearn Herald* reported that work was likely to begin in a few days time. A few days later it was able to report that operations were being pushed rapidly forward and several large sheds had been constructed for storing materials. The first lot of navvies' huts had been placed at the back of the village and it was expected that the undertaking would be finished in about two years time. In July it was reported that ground had been broken at Laggan and the Mill of Ross.

An unfortunate hiccup occurred when the contractor cut down an avenue of 100-year-old plane trees, running from the Lednock towards Lawers, that had been planted by Colonel Williamson's grandfather and which they had assured him were not in the line of the railway. The Colonel was furious and neither forgot nor forgave him for this.

In the same month the foundations were laid for the railway bridge across the Lednock and preparations were made for building the massive bridge at the other end of the village across the Earn. The weather that summer and autumn was very favourable and the work was pushed ahead rapidly.

In August the public road opposite the station was diverted so that work could begin on extending the railway under the road. A large gravel knoll in Laggan Park was utilised in building the rising embankment behind the village and a stone-breaking machine was erected in the station yard. The navvies were also busy constructing the line further west at the Mill of Ross.

One unfortunate casualty of the railway was Mrs Arnott, the widow of David 'Miller' Arnott who had worked the meal mill on the banks of the Lednock for decades until its closure in the 1880s. Now a 96-year-old widow, the cottage she had lived in for 65 years stood in the way of the railway and she was moved to another location where she died only a few weeks later. The old mill building itself was largely demolished and its stones were used in constructing the railway.

As if the engineering works on the line were not enough of a problem, the contractor also had to deal with a letter from the Bishop of St Andrews asking for subscriptions to support the services of a missionary to labour amongst the navvies working on the line. This provoked an animated correspondence in the *Strathearn Herald*, during which it emerged that Colonel Williamson was behind the project. Opponents of the scheme contended that with two established church and three dissenting clergymen already resident in the parish, there were sufficient moral resources to cater for the needs of the navvies. But the Colonel and the Bishop replied that 'navvies are men of peculiar habits and will respond better to someone who understands them and can direct their thoughts to a settled manner of life and of the life to come'.

As usual the Colonel had his way and a missionary from the Scottish Navvy Mission was duly appointed at a salary of £84 per year. It was subsequently reported that the missionary was doing good work, speaking on spiritual subjects, advising men in difficulties and writing letters to their friends.

It was reported that the village shopkeepers were now extremely busy with navvies and tourists. The navvies were said to be extremely well-behaved when sober, some having their wages deposited in the local Savings Bank whilst others had joined the Water Drinking Society. Religious services were held near their huts every Sunday and plans were in hand to erect a reading room for them.

This picture of the navvies is a far cry from the traditional image of the railway navvy of 50 years earlier who lived in a shanty town and, together with his mates, went on a drunken 'randy' whenever he was paid. All the same, in spite of these encouraging reports about the navvies' exemplary conduct, most issues of the *Strathearn Herald* over the next two years contain reports of two or three of them every week being brought before the Sheriff Court in Perth on charges of drunkenness, assault, theft or violent behaviour. Their usual punishment was a fine with the option of imprisonment for several days.

When the line was being built between Crieff and Comrie there had been very little comment in the local newspapers about the conduct of the navvies, other than to say that they were well behaved, well looked after and properly housed by the contractor. Six years later this idyllic situation had now changed completely.

Occasionally their behaviour had fatal consequences. In October an Irish navvy named John Gallagher was found dead at the side of the railway line about half a mile on the Crieff side of Comrie station. He had severe injuries and it was believed that he had lain down to sleep too close to the line and had been hit by a train.

The navvies' image was further tarnished by a report that recommended the establishment of a reading room because,

. . . the sight of these men wandering aimlessly about the village after working hours is inexpressibly sad. The disgraceful state of the streets crowded with drunken men is not to be wondered at when one knows that the poor fellows have only the public houses to fall back upon for rest and refreshment.

The navvies' Reading Room, sponsored by Colonel Williamson, was duly opened in September 1899. It was especially appreciated by the navvies during the coming winter months as a place where they could relax in front of a warm fire and dry their sodden clothes.

But by the following April the *Strathearn Herald* was reporting, under the heading 'Notes from Comrie - Navvies and Drink', that:

Navvies lying helplessly intoxicated during the week has been a common sight on our streets and highways during the winter, but it is only during the past month that they have included Sunday. On Sabbath last, on the outskirts of the village, a number of these worthies were to be found lying helpless through drink, advantage being taken, no doubt, of the Act which allows a refreshment at any hotel should the applicant have travelled three miles. More than a refreshment had been got in these cases as, besides being helplessly drunk, they still had in their possession a bottle of a renowned Highland brand full to the bung. The seller had been careful not to have the name of his hotel figuring on the label. How to stop this trafficking in liquor on the Sabbath Day is a nice point for the Licensing Board, and one which should have their attention at the forthcoming half-yearly Court. When the navvies first came to the village all manner of stories were current as to their ability as thieves and housebreakers, but up to the present not one case of theft or housebreaking of a serious nature has been reported to the Police. No small amount of credit is due to the local police for their vigilance and attention to duty. Although not a member or a subscriber to the Navvy Mission, a hint for their future guidance may not come amiss, - viz instead of a missionary, provide and pay two stalwart men to lift the poor fellows off the street and escort them safely to their huts. I (says a correspondent) have seen the poor chaps lying helplessly drunk by the side of the highway on a cold and stormy night and, but for the good offices of the local police and some good-hearted civilians, many would have perished. The Comrie people don't dislike the navvy and will help him when occasion permits, but they are under the impression that the Navvy Mission, if it wants to do some good, should adopt some other course than the one in force. By the way, the different clerics vied with each other at the commencement of the railway in holding services at the navvies' huts but this is now a thing of the past.

In August a visitor to the village wrote to the *Strathearn Herald* that around 6 o'clock on a Saturday evening he had been travelling from St Fillans to Comrie by coach and had passed six navvies who were dead drunk, some lying by the roadside, as well as several others who were obviously under the influence of liquor. He questioned whether the whisky and beer served in the village was up to legal standards or whether it was adulterated.

This letter provoked a vigorous response from Colonel Williamson in his capacity as Chairman of the Licensing Committee. He quoted a letter he had received from the Chief Constable which certified that spot-checks carried out in the village's hotels and bars showed that beers and spirits sold locally were indeed of the legal standard. In the Colonel's opinion, the problem was due to the navvies' immense appetite for beer which they liberally mixed with glasses of whisky during the course of a drinking session.

By November 1899 the road bridge over the railway by Comrie station was almost completed and the stone piers of the railway bridge over the Lednock had been finished and were ready for the erection of their girders. The embankment of sand and rough stone running behind the village was ready for the rails to be laid and the viaduct at its west end was almost complete.

This viaduct was a massive structure of 11 masonry arches with two separate girder sections which spanned Dundas Street and the River Earn respectively. The masonry abutments either side of Dundas Street were of red sandstone and 7 feet thick. Those either side of the Earn were 8 ft thick whilst the intermediate piers were 5 feet thick.

By now the line had been formed for a further half mile towards St Fillans and work was well advanced on excavating the large cutting beyond, whilst the abutments of the second bridge across the Earn near Tullybannocher Smiddy were ready to receive their girders. Mr Paton reported that he hoped to have an engine running for one or two miles by the end of the year.

A local newspaper reported that:

Next summer the new railway from Comrie to St Fillans will be in full working order. The route followed has been a difficult one to work. A great quantity of rock has had to be displaced but all obstacles are gradually being overcome and the present state of the work is generally considered satisfactory.

From Comrie station the line proceeds round the north, or back, of the town, crosses Dundas Street on a bridge of several arches, and continues into the open country, through the Ross lands, in a westerly direction under the shade of the Aberuchill Hills. No fewer than four bridges cross the Earn on the first five mile stretch of line. The first of these is situated behind the main street of Comrie, the second at Tullybannocher, the third near Dalchonzie, and the fourth and last at Tynreoch, close to Dundurn wooden bridge. A comparatively new method is being followed in the construction of these bridges: they are made of concrete. On portions of the route the rails are already laid and ballasting and sleepers are down for a considerable length. Most of the cuttings which have had to be made were formed of solid rock, and blasting has had to be resorted to in every case. Probably the heaviest piece of work is at present, and will be for some time to come, a long ridge of rock in Dunira Wood, close to the River Earn, where extensive blasting and excavation is going on. At St. Fillans the station is being built slightly to the west of Littleport farm-steading.

Concrete had first been used extensively in railway building by Sir Robert McAlpine when he built the extension of the West Highland Railway from Fort William to Mallaig between 1897 and 1901. It proved so successful that he used it on other major contracts and acquired the nickname of 'Concrete Bob'.

Work resumed in January 1900 after a break for Christmas and New Year holidays, and a number of navvy huts were moved further down the line towards St Fillans. In March the Reading Room was relocated from Comrie to Tynreoch and the missionary relocated with it. By now this gentleman was not receiving much support from the public who had been asked by the Navvy Mission to contribute £55 by the end of November; by the middle of August they had contributed exactly £10.

The railway bridge over the Lednock at Comrie was opened on 18th April by Colonel Williamson who drove the contractor's 'pug' engine across it.

In June the Caledonian decided that Comrie station needed to be converted into a double-platformed station for convenience in working the through trains between Crieff and Balquhidder. This necessitated purchasing more land from Colonel Williamson so its Traffic Department lost no time in getting in touch with him.

Unfortunately for them, the man they were now dealing with was not the enthusiastic crusader of a few years previously. They were now faced with a great landowner who had virtually bankrupted his estate in fulfilling his ambition of bringing the railway to Comrie and who was now going to extract the full market price for giving up any more of his land in the interest of further expansion westwards.

Eventually they paid Colonel Williamson £1,000 for the portion of his land they had taken. £315 was then spent on constructing the up platform and its buildings, namely a booking office, waiting room and signal box.

But that was not the end of the matter. When it came to the question of access, Colonel Williamson demanded a further £315 for an approach road to the new platform. Negotiations dragged on for nearly a year before the Colonel agreed to settle for £200, which included him constructing and fencing the approach roadway and also giving a small amount of land for a dead-end siding.

In July it was reported that work was progressing well and that most of the contractor's plant was being moved nearer to St Fillans. The rising embankment from the Lednock to Dundas Street had been completed and the navvies were now mostly located at the St Fillans end of the line. The most difficult part of the work was excavating the large rock cutting in Dunira Wood adjoining the Earn.

The Directors were obviously keeping up the pressure on the contractor because Mr Paton wrote to Colonel Williamson in November 1900 saying that he did not intend to start the Lednock road bridge for another month or two and until the steelwork was forward. He said that this was not suitable work to commence in the dead of winter and he did not see why he should do so when it might have been done the previous summer if he had been allowed to get on with it. (This was obviously a reference to the delay caused by the Colonel's dispute with the District Council over the siting of the bridge.)

In a further letter to Colonel Williamson in December (sent to him at the Talbot Hotel, Malton, where he was enjoying the hunting season), Mr Paton said he would be starting work shortly on building the service bridge. Its erection would only take about a week but he did not want to start until the girders were ready so that the interference with traffic would be for as short a time as possible. Also, the weather of late had been lamentable, with heavy rain every day.

By the end of March a service road had been built to the south of the old Lednock bridge which was now in course of demolition. Work progressed swiftly and on 8th June Colonel Williamson formally opened the present bridge by driving over it in his pony trap.

On the railway, all the principal bridges were practically complete and the rails had been laid and ballasted almost the whole way to St Fillans apart from in the Dunira rock cutting which was now almost finished. St Fillans station was being built with two platforms, the offices and waiting rooms being located on the westbound platform and constructed in terra-cotta brickwork, timber and rough-cast plaster work with red-tiled roof. The platforms and retaining walls were of concrete. A goods yard with shed, loading bank and sidings was being constructed on the north side of the station.

By the end of June the contractor's engines were able to work the full length of the line to St Fillans but it was not until 6th September that it was ready for Colonel Van Donop to inspect on behalf of the Board of Trade, using two heavy engines for testing bridges and permanent way.

The inspection was satisfactory and on 12th September a special train carrying Directors and railway officials was run from Glasgow to St Fillans, picking up a contingent of press reporters at Comrie. The train, which made several stops between Comrie and St Fillans for photography and viewing of engineering highlights, comprised two saloon coaches hauled by the famous 4-2-2 'Single' No. 123 which had worked the Caledonian Railway's section (between Carlisle and Edinburgh) of the 1888 'Railway Race to the North'.

The first timetable showed passenger trains arriving at St Fillans at 7.08 am, 12.17 pm and 6.10 pm with departures at 8.05 am, 1.25 pm and 6.15 pm. Most trains ran to and from Glasgow and Edinburgh.

St Fillans station looking east, shortly before the line from Comrie opened in 1901. The island (up) platform has not yet been completed although its paved edging is in place, and the billboards do not display any posters. A contractor's machine and workmen can be seen in the background.

National Railway Museum/STR 495

The public service began inauspiciously on 1st October when the first train of the day had great difficulty, in wet weather, in climbing the gradient from Comrie station up to the Dundas Street bridge. Apart from that, everything went smoothly and a large number of passengers travelled on the new line on its opening day.

Two days later a minor mishap occurred at St Fillans when the engine shunting wagons for the 2.30 pm goods train to Perth was derailed in the goods yard and caused a considerable amount of damage to the tracks. A breakdown crane was sent out from Perth and its crew worked through the night to re-rail the engine and restore the track.

But a familiar problem now arose. The Lochearnhead company had run out of money! As early as November 1898 a Special Meeting of the shareholders of the new railway had been held to decide what action to take in the event of their share of the capital not being fully subscribed. On 21st March, 1899, the Caledonian's General Manager had reported to his Board that he had had an interview with that railway's chairman, Colonel Home-Drummond, in which the latter had asked that the Caledonian should take over the undertaking entirely. His request was noted but the Board resolved to take no action for the present.

Less than three months later the new railway's Secretary had again written to the Caledonian's Board, this time asking them to advance them money for the purchase of land along the railway's route.

When the company's shares had been floated on the Stock Market in February 1899 the investing public had shown very little interest in the project and subscribed for only a small proportion of the rest of the capital. This situation was not lost on the Caledonian who had already subscribed 50 per cent (£87,500) of the capital themselves.

By the time the railway had been built almost as far as St Fillans the money had run out and the Lochearnhead company was unable to raise its share of the capital. With a further 9½ miles still to go to connect up with the Callander & Oban, the Caledonian was faced with the stark choice of either abandoning its investment altogether or taking over the construction of the railway itself. It decided to confront the inevitable and on 7th May, 1901, Henry Stirling Home-Drummond and David Robertson Williamson, Directors, and Thomas Dempster, Secretary of the Lochearnhead, St Fillans & Comrie Railway Company signed an Agreement with the Caledonian Railway Company. The Caledonian formally took over the bankrupt company as from 1st August, 1902 and advanced money in the meantime to continue the work.

As we have seen, the railway was opened from Comrie to St Fillans on 1st October, 1901. A few months before the line was completed, tenders had been invited from contractors for the second stage of the line, the 9½ miles from St Fillans to join the Callander & Oban line at Balquhidder, which it was reckoned would take about 2½ years to complete. Several contractors submitted tenders and the contract was again awarded to John Paton & Co. Its tender of £113,000 was not the lowest but the Directors were evidently pleased with his work on the Comrie to St Fillans line and showed their confidence in him.

A problem arose further down the line. Lady Helen MacGregor of Edinchip had tried to prevent the railway surveyors entering onto her land without first buying it or coming under an obligation to purchase it whether the railway went ahead or not. The matter came before the Sheriff and she eventually lost her case.

Lady Helen MacGregor continued to be troublesome and demanded that the company should deposit a substantial part of the £5,500 compensation she claimed. She was offered £1,750 but it was a further two years before her claim was settled by arbitration at £2,024. In June 1904 she made a further claim, this time for payment of £250 in lieu of providing an overbridge, which appears to have been paid.

The Earl of Ancaster proved equally troublesome. Initially he had claimed £4,000 for the purchase of his lands east of St Fillans but he increased this to £4,392. Now he claimed a further £6,250 for his lands west of St Fillans plus £900 in lieu of the company providing accommodation bridges over its line. After these amounts had been paid to him, he made a further claim in March 1904 for £400 in lieu of the company providing an overbridge at Littleport; this was settled for £350. And in March 1905 they settled a further claim for £242.

Still not satisfied, his Lordship claimed additional compensation for 'the want and insufficiency of level crossings' on his land. This claim was settled for £250.

At the Comrie end of the line Sir Sidney Dundas claimed £6,000 for the portion of his land required for the railway whilst the major landowner at the other end of the line, the Marquis of Breadalbane, claimed the value of his land to be £7,000 but offered to settle for £4,750.

The attitude shown towards this railway by the great landowners west of Comrie was in marked contrast to attitude of the majority of landowners along the line of the Crieff & Comrie Railway a few years earlier when Colonel Williamson had been personally trying so hard to get them to be public-spirited. It is hard to avoid the impression that they were trying to get every penny they could out of the Caledonian which was, at that time, the wealthiest railway company in Scotland.

Work on the second contract had commenced in June 1901 but was thrown into confusion only six months later when John Paton unexpectedly died of a chill on 27th January, 1902 at the age of only 40. He had set up in business around 1889 after gaining railway experience on building the Caledonian's Killin and Airdrie lines and the Lochearnhead line had been his biggest contract.

Work on the railway was immediately suspended whilst another contractor could be found who would complete the contract. In the meantime the navvies were out of work and starving; within a week the workforce dropped from 493 to around 80. Most of the navvies left to find other work but soon began to drift back because the severe weather had caused other works in Scotland to be stopped.

On 16th February a church collection was taken at St Fillans for the benefit of the navvies. With the money raised from this and other local subscriptions, the Revd Armstrong and his wife opened a soup kitchen. Mr Carmichael at the St Fillans Hotel provided bread and soup (replaced by herring and potatoes on Friday for the benefit of the many Irish Catholic navvies) and surplus funds were used to provide rail tickets for navvies wanting to move permanently away to other locations. In all, the soup kitchen was open for 16 days and 36 men were provided with rail tickets.

Eventually the contract was taken over by the Glasgow firm of William Duncan who, like their predecessor, continued to work under the supervision of the Caledonian.

By the summer of 1902 between 300 and 400 navvies were again working on the line and it was hoped to have two or three miles completed by the autumn. The Navvy Mission Hall was relocated to Glentarken but was poorly supported by the public; it was reckoned to cost £100 per year to maintain but subscriptions by the end of July only amounted to £5 5s. Drunkenness amongst the navvies was still a problem but this had now been transferred to the banks of Loch Earn. Even as late as May 1904 the Superintendent was appealing for books, magazines and newspapers ('which need not be new'), particularly religious and secular illustrated magazines, for the Mission House so that the navvies could while away the time after work or on wet days without having to resort to the nearest public house for their entertainment.

Contemporary newspaper reports make reference to an aerial ropeway known as 'Blondin Tackle'. One or two thick wires were slung between two posts set a considerable distance apart and large buckets which looked like huge coal scuttles ran along them, suspended from small pulley hooks. The navvies working in a cutting would fill the buckets with earth and the contents were taken along the ropeway and deposited into waggons which took them further along the line to where they were dumped to form an embankment.

Rock drills operated by steam power, another feature of modern railway construction at this time, were also used in constructing this section of the line.

With the railway now almost completed, the St Fillans Curling Club held a banquet at the Ancaster Arms Hotel in Comrie on 28th April, 1904 for the officials who had been involved in constructing the line and were now about to leave the area. Revd Armstrong was in the chair and, proposing a toast to 'The Railwaymen', spoke of the happy times they had spent together on St Fillans Curling Pond. In response, Mr Robertson (inspector of works) and Mr Duncan (contractor) said they would never forget the kindness they had met from their friends in the Comrie and St Fillans districts.

This section of the line had taken nearly three years to build. A special inspection train containing railway officials and reporters from the national newspapers was run on 15th June, 1904, again comprising two saloon coaches headed by No. 123, but it was not until 1st July that the railway opened for passenger traffic through to Lochearnhead. It subsequently opened for freight traffic on 18th July and Mr Duncan was awarded a £250 bonus.

A few weeks before the official opening to Lochearnhead the *Strathearn Herald* described the new line in the following terms:

Starting at Balquhidder Junction, where the line will join the Callander & Oban Railway, where extensive operations are at present in progress by way of preparing for the construction of new and commodious station premises for the accommodation of the passenger and goods traffic which will be exchanged between the Callander & Oban Railway and the Lochearnhead and Crieff line. The present station structure - platforms, offices, sheds, etc. are to be swept away and the new and enlarged station and its passenger platforms will be placed about 170 yards westward from the present position, so as to facilitate the junction between the two railways. The whole of the works at the

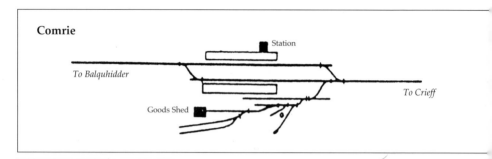

Comrie

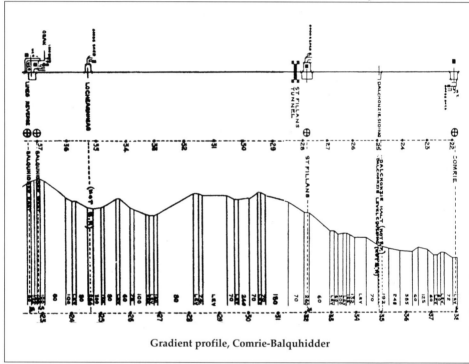

Gradient profile, Comrie-Balquhidder

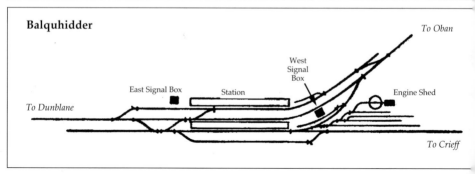

Balquhidder

Publicity photographs of the extension to Balquhidder, 1905.   *J. MacIntosh*

The island platform at Balquhidder looking towards Stirling in Caledonian Railway days. The poster is advertising the Loch Tay steamer service to Kenmore which passengers would have reached via Killin Junction and the branch train from there to the steamer pier at Killin. All were owned by the Caledonian Railway.   *R.M. Casserley*

Balquhidder station and post office *c.*1905. The buildings on the down platform are on the right of the picture with the West signal box beyond them and the engine shed in the distance. The post office is now a restaurant and all the other buildings have long-since been demolished.
A. Cameron

station involve a considerable lowering of the present levels, including a portion of the Callander and Oban line. The goods department is to be placed a considerable distance east of the passenger station. The public road leading from Lochearnhead to Balquhidder and Callander, which closely adjoins the station, has for a stretch of 300 or 400 yards been diverted some distance northward, and the Callander & Oban line will also for a slight distance undergo a slight deviation in the same direction. It may likewise be noted that four or five neat cottages in picturesque situations have been erected on both sides of the road, a little to the west of the station, for the accommodation of the railway servants, and some of these are already occupied. Returning to the station works, it may be mentioned that the island platform design having been adopted, necessitated the construction of a subway for foot passengers, as the public road is about 12 feet lower than platform level. Under the platform, arches are constructed, and under the main line, stamped steel flooring, filled with concrete, has been set. The subway is built throughout of 6 to 1 concrete faced, where covered, with white enamelled bricks and, where exposed, the facing is 4 to 1 concrete. All the walls are finished on top with 14 by 9 splayed red stone coping, which considerably relieves the dead look such a mass of concrete would otherwise have. At present the general works in connection with the station are practically confined to cutting and banking, and rapid progress is being made with the excavations.

From the station downwards for a distance of about three-quarters of a mile, the railway runs on the south side of the public highway leading to Lochearnhead through a stretch of moorland and moss, and distant from the road 40 to 100 yards. It is satisfactory to note that over this stretch of three-quarters of a mile the permanent rails are already laid and that portion of the line completed. The gradient here for some distance is a pretty heavy one, being 1 in 60. In connection with the work of constructing of the line, although comparatively little excavation work appears to have been necessary, there are one or two points of interest that may be described. Immediately on leaving the station, after passing through a small cutting, a bank of about 10 chains long is formed on the top of moss, and an interesting method has been adopted to prevent subsidence. For the first three months after the bank had been completed, rapid subsidence was noticeable, but since the last filling up of the parts subsided, about four months ago, no appreciable sinking has been detected. About the middle of the moss stretch, it was found necessary to build what is known as a 'cattle creep'.*

Some three-quarters of a mile from Lochearnhead Junction the line curves round to the north side of the public road crossing that thoroughfare by a high-level bridge, the road here being diverted for some little distance to the north, at a point almost opposite Edinchip mansion house. The bridge carrying the line across the road forms part of what is known as Edinchip viaduct which spans the Ceanndroma Water and the valley through which it rushes on its course down to Loch Earn. The viaduct is one of the heaviest portions of work on the whole of the railway, and will entail great labour and much expense. It is about 56 feet high and will consist of seven arches of 40 feet span and one 80 feet girder span over the stream. The piers and arches are constructed wholly of concrete, and already considerable progress has been made with the work. After leaving the viaduct nothing special of note is met with - the line passing along the lower slopes of the hill through layers of slatey rock, etc. - until fully a mile onwards. At this point the line, as originally set out, was to run through a deep cutting, but after the gullet had been taken out for three or four chains, the nature of the material was such that, at the suggestion of the contractor, the engineer agreed to shift the centre about 7 feet down the hill at the deepest point of the cutting and, in this way, save a large outlay in drainage. This suggestion was the more readily agreed to as great expense had been incurred in connection with a cutting of the same description near St. Fillans. This adjustment of the centre line being just at the west entrance to Lochearnhead station, caused some alteration on the main line through the station. The run along this portion

* Author's explanatory note: A 'cattle creep' is a narrow bridge sufficiently wide to allow cattle to pass under the railway embankment from fields on one side of the line to the other but not wide enough for vehicular traffic

Balquhidder: the main line inner face of the up island platform looking south-east towards Callander, *c.*1905.   *National Railway Museum/LGRP 24575*

Balquhidder: branch train for the Crieff line standing at the outer face of the island platform headed by McIntosh 0-4-4T No. 439, *c.*1905. The sacks in the foreground appear to contain fleeces.   *National Railway Museum/LGRP 7976*

of the line to the station is on an almost level track and, just at the head of Loch Earn, a magnificent prospect of the entire width of which is obtained from the line,

Lochearnhead Station, which is in course of being constructed, is very prettily and romantically, situated just at the back of the hotel and skirting the base of the hill. Walking along the platform, one is face to face with the whole expanse of the wild and rugged mountain scenery which stretches from Edinchip on the south to Glenogle on the north; whilst some 300 yards or so straight up the mountain side, terraced amongst rocks and heather, is the Callander & Oban Railway. The whole of the slopes at the station, being of a gravelly nature and somewhat wet, these have been turfed instead of soiling, as has been done over most of the other slopes, and certainly it will enhance the natural beauty in the immediate vicinity of the station which has an additional feature, in the form of a natural cascade which rushes down the mountain side at the south end of the platform. The station itself will not only be very commodious - and is designed with ample provision for future requirements - but will be so constructed as to harmonise with its beautiful surroundings. The platform, extending in all to a little under 200 yards, is of the island description. The entrance to the station will be off the Glenogle road at the west side of the hotel stables, and the platform is approached by a subway similar to that at Lochearnhead Junction - concrete lined with white enamel bricks. On the stairs here a wooden covering is to be erected so that the subway will always be kept thoroughly dry.

The goods shed, etc., will be placed at the west end of the station. The loading bank, of which 90 feet is on the level and 90 feet on a gradient of 1 in 20, is faced with a concrete wall 3 feet thick at the bottom and 2 feet thick at the top, and finished at 3 feet 6 inches above rail level with a 12 x 6 inch creosoted red pine cope. On the east side of the Glenogle road, opposite the entrance to the station road, several cottages have been erected for the accommodation of the stationmasters and porters.

From Lochearnhead station the line curves round towards the east, crosses the Glenogle road, and immediately enters upon the Glenogle Viaduct, the largest and most important feature of the railway. The viaduct, which bridges the entrance to Glenogle, consists of 9 arches of 40 feet spans and was built in the autumn of last year. The viaduct, like all the other works on the railway, has been wholly constructed of concrete, on account of the want of suitable building stone in the district and the great expense of bringing stones from a distance. The viaduct is a huge and substantial-looking structure and forms a conspicuous object in the landscape. From this point onwards the railway runs along the hill slope on the north side of Loch Earn at distances varying from 100 to 250 yards from the loch and the public road which skirts it, and from a height of 100 feet above the level of the water for 6½ miles over which the loch extends. Some two miles eastwards from Lochearnhead the line passes through the croft-lands of the estate of Lord Breadalbane and numerous gates, pathways, bridges, etc. have had to be provided to afford convenient access to the upper portions of the crofts. The slope between the railway and the public road is here almost devoid of any trees, and a full and uninterrupted view of the loch is obtained. The other four to five miles of the railway journey, however, is made through an almost continuous thicket of oak copse, while at Glentarken there is quite a little forest of pretty young larch. But the railway track is sufficiently exalted to ensure - even in summer when foliage is thickest - delightful glimpses of the bosom of the loch; while on the south side the lofty summit of Ben Vorlich is seen cut in majestic outline against the horizon; and the quaint towers of Edinample Castle and the picturesquely situated mansion of Ardvorlich are also conspicuous on the southern shores of Loch Earn.

Amongst further features of the work of construction of the line until it reaches St Fillans which may be referred to is a bridge at Glenbeich, and where there is a considerable length of valley at the mouth of the valley. The valley has been banked, while a bridge over the Beich Burn and road bridge combined have been built, the skew span of which is fully 38 feet between the two piers, each 8 feet thick. Some distance eastward there is another girder bridge with an 80 feet span. The line at various points,

An eastbound train, headed by a McIntosh 0-4-4 tank engine running bunker-first, about to cross the viaduct at Lochearnhead in 1904. The large building in the middle of the picture is the old Lochearnhead Hotel which was later destroyed by fire. The station roof can be seen above the trees to its left and the line of trees running horizontally across the hillside marks the course of the Callander & Oban Railway as it climbs northwards into Glen Ogle.   *A. Cameron*

A panoramic view of Lochearnhead station in 1904. The cutting and new bridge on the left of the picture shows that work is underway on the final two miles to link up with the Callander & Oban Railway. The horizontal line of trees on the hillside marks the latter's course down to Balquhidder where the two lines will meet at the new Balquhidder Junction station.

A. Cameron

The newly-built Lochearnhead station ready for its opening on 1st July 1904. The magnificent nine-arch viaduct in the background carried the line across the southern approach to Glen Ogle and was built entirely of concrete. *A. Cameron*

Lochearnhead station and goods yard in 1905 when the final two miles of line to Balquhidder had been completed. *A. Cameron*

A postcard *c.*1905 showing Lochearnhead station with Loch Earn itself in the background.
J. MacIntosh

Lochearnhead station in 1905 looking towards Comrie with the signal box prominent.
Perth & Kinross Museum W487

for several miles, has a good many stiff gradients and a few sharp curves in getting round rocky knolls, notwithstanding the extensive blasting there must have been in cutting the track through the mountainous region. Near the farmhouse of Derry - immediately behind which the line passes - we come to another span of three arches. Then opposite Derry is a picturesque open space from which a lovely vista is obtained. Here is an ideal spot on which to build, and were the Railway Company to establish a side station at this point - as has, we believe, been contemplated - there is no doubt but that it would be speedily feued by the Earl of Ancaster, whose property it is. At Glentarken, further down, another pretty open space is passed. Here there has been a good deal of heavy banking and rock cutting, and several costly bridges including a very high level one across a deep gorge, down through which passes a turbulent mountain stream close to Woodhouse. A short distance eastwards the line traverses one of the most extensive embankments in its whole course, and one which has caused so much trouble and no little expense. The bank is formed on side lying ground, of such inclination that it was decided to build a dry-stone retaining wall about 30 feet, parallel to the centre line. The wall was built, and the banking put in, but the wall burst in several places, causing the bank to slip. The bank was afterwards filled up with ashes, and with the addition of numerous rumbling drains along the north side of the line, the bank has now been rendered secure. About a mile from St. Fillans the work of construction has been of a very expensive nature. Several big streams in their course down the hillside to the loch and deep gorges had to be bridged, and at one point no fewer than five arches span one of these gorges; while at two other points there are other streams that had to be spanned with three and two arches respectively. One or two overhead bridges are also erected here and a new service hill road made at a point near the west end of St. Fillans

Coming now to the tunnel at St. Fillans, it extends in all to 62 lineal yards. It is entirely through rock, and of such good quality was this that in three-quarters of the length no excavation timber was found necessary. The interior of the tunnel is lined with concrete, 18 inches thick. The tunnel, it may be mentioned, was not provided for in the original design, but in order to partly preserve the amenity of the villa residences in the immediate vicinity and upper part of the village, it was subsequently decided to tunnel this part of the face of the hill. Needless to say, the railway from the vantage ground overlooking St. Fillans affords a magnificent prospect of the entire length of Loch Earn and the mountain ranges on either side.

The rock on this final half-mile to St Fillans was mainly schistose with occasional dykes of whin. One of these dykes was encountered just before the station and proved a very tough job to blast but the stone provided excellent ballast for the track.

It was anticipated that the final two miles to Balquhidder would be open before the end of that year but unexpected engineering difficulties were encountered on the last mile, which was veritable bog. Not only did the morass have no foundation but the rainfall that year was no less than 110 inches. In the end the engineers had to dig a cutting about 30 feet wide through the bog until they reached the level of the original earth. They then built a strong embankment of stone, earth and ballast in the cutting to bring the line up to the surface level.

The final stretch of line did not open until 1st May, 1905, the day *before* the official Board of Trade inspection on which the special blue and gold officers' saloon, drawn by 'Single' No. 123, was used. There was no formal opening ceremony and, because the line had not yet been inspected, a planned inaugural excursion train from Aberdeen to Oban via the new line had to be re-routed via Dunblane and Callander instead.

Another official photo of a train and station staff at St Fillans in 1901. The billboards are advertising the Caledonian's services to Belfast, from Glasgow and Edinburgh to the North and their Clyde Coast services to Wemyss Bay and Gourock.

National Railway Museum/STR 497

The bridge over the River Earn at Tynreoch, east of St Fillans, in 1904.

National Railway Museum/STR 504

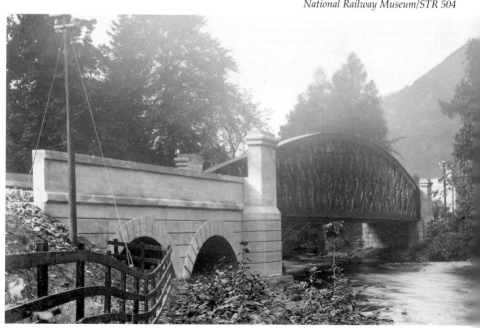

The Caledonian Railway's famous 4-2-2 'Single' No. 123 poses on the Earn viaduct at Comrie on 12th September, 1901 with a special train conveying Directors, railway officials and members of the press to St Fillans. The nearest steel span carries the line over the River Earn and the further one over Dundas Street, with the former East Free Church of 1866 close by.
National Railway Museum/STR 181

The special train seen further down the line towards St Fillans, posing on the concrete viaduct at Dundurn.   *National Railway Museum/STR 182*

A three-coach westbound train headed by a McIntosh 0-4-4 tank engine crossing the Edinchip viaduct between Lochearnhead and Balquhidder *c*.1905.   *A. Cameron*

An eastbound train, headed by a McIntosh 0-4-4 tank engine, leaving Lochearnhead viaduct *c*.1905.   *A. Cameron*

The whole line was quite heavily graded, the ruling gradient being about 1 in 60. Travelling westwards and leaving St Fillans at a height of about 130 feet above the level of the loch, the line descended to the point where it crossed the Beich Burn at only 40 feet above the loch. It then climbed again to around 100 feet before dropping again to cross Glen Ogle on the curved Lochearnhead viaduct with its nine arches of 40 ft span. This viaduct had been the subject of an enquiry by a Committee of Taste of the House of Commons regarding its effect on the beauty of the neighbourhood and especially the view up and down Glen Ogle.

Very soon after leaving the viaduct, the island platform of Lochearnhead station was reached. Here it was customary to check the tickets of passengers bound for Balquhidder and beyond on the Callander & Oban line.

At this point on the line the railway was quite close to the Callander & Oban line but at a considerably lower level. The final two miles to Balquhidder Junction were at a steeply rising gradients of 1 in 80, 1 in 100 and finally 1 in 60, and involved crossing the Channdroma Water by a seven-arched viaduct of 40 ft span and a steel girder of 80 ft span.

Balquhidder station had originally been named Lochearnhead, despite being about a mile distant from the village. It was rebuilt on a site 170 yards to the west and was renamed Balquhidder Junction in March 1904 when the separate station (with freight facilities) was opened at Lochearnhead on the newly-completed line from Comrie.

From being a wayside station Balquhidder became a junction with an engine shed, a turntable and two signal boxes, the West with 36 levers and the East with 45 levers. The permanent staff of one station master, one signalman and one porter was increased by three signalmen, one porter-guard and one porter. The waiting room was used for a time as a council chamber by Balquhidder Parish Council and as a polling station at local and general elections.

At the new Balquhidder Junction an 800 ft long and 45 ft wide island platform was constructed west of the old station on the up side so that the trains arriving from the Crieff & Comrie direction could be handled on its outer face. Double tracks were laid on either side of the platform and extended some way beyond them. There was a single platform on the down side with the engine shed and sidings adjacent. Callander & Oban main line trains used this for northbound trains and the inner face of the island platform for southbound trains.

One obvious disadvantage of this arrangement, from the point of view of the Lochearnhead line, is that trains from their line destined for Oban had to reverse here. That is probably the reason why their earliest thoughts, as illustrated by Mr Young's sketch map (*see page 72*), showed their line turning north-west at Glen Ogle and making a trailing connection with the Callander & Oban line somewhere near Killin Junction.

Comrie station was enlarged when it became a through station. In March 1903 a pipe was laid from the gas mains and the lamp was re-sited to give better lighting on the access road. In June 1905 a second platform was constructed for eastbound trains.

Comrie, St Fillans and Lochearnhead were the only intermediate stations on the new line but a platform was constructed at Dalchonzie (between Comrie and St Fillans) at which trains called conditionally on passengers giving notice to the guard at the previous station. The line crossed a minor road on the level at this point and the crossing was controlled by gates operated from a signal box

McIntosh 4-6-0 No. 52 approaching St Fillans tunnel eastbound with the Royal Train. The occasion is thought to have been in either 1905 or 1909. The locomotive is not carrying the royal headcode so the King himself may not have been on board at the time.

J.F. McEwan, courtesy of Dunbartonshire Information & Archives

opposite the platform. The signal box also controlled access to a siding, the only one on the line apart from those at the station yards, and incorporated houses for the two signalmen who worked the box. The platform was opened on 15th July, 1903 and in November the Company spent £6 on installing three lamps. It was not until July 1906 that a shelter was erected at a cost of £55 but, even so, it remained a rather bleak spot to the end of its days.

In an attempt to encourage passengers to visit the countryside that had now been opened up by the new railway the Caledonian began running a special Saturday afternoon express between Perth and Balquhidder, a round journey of 77 miles for a price of 1s. 6d.

A tragic accident occurred in August 1904 about 100 yards east of Dalchonzie crossing. Twenty-seven-year-old Mrs Smith and her two young children, family of the overseer of the Dunira Estate, lived in a cottage on the south side of the line which was connected to the main road on the north side of the railway by a small footpath. On this occasion the mother had crossed the line to purchase supplies from a baker's van on the main road when she noticed that her youngest daughter, aged 20 months, had wandered after her and was standing on the track. She immediately rushed to retrieve her but both were struck and killed by the 2 pm train from Crieff to St Fillans.

One local business that does appear to have profited from the building of the line was the Comrie firm of Peter Comrie & Sons. The Caledonian Railway's minutes record him as having constructed the following (and possibly more) buildings:

Station master's House, St Fillans	£350
Two Cottages at Lochearnhead	
Station master's House, Lochearnhead	£510
Railwaymen's Houses, Lochearnhead	£560
Lochearnhead Station Buildings	£1,266
Lochearnhead Goods Shed	£375
Lochearnhead Signal Cabin	£279
Balquhidder Station Island Platform buildings and verandah	£1,029
Balquhidder South Signal Cabin	£243

However, Peter did not have it all to himself. The Caledonian Railway's minutes show that Robert McRobbie was paid £320 for building cottages at St Fillans and William Spry was paid £1,019 for building cottages at the new Balquhidder Junction. In addition, Messrs Cowan, Shildon & Co. were paid £485 for a new turntable at Balquhidder whilst, at the other end of the line, a water column was installed at Crieff for £288 and additional engine shed accommodation for £180.

Back in Comrie Village, in January 1907 the Revd John Macpherson wrote to the Caledonian Directors, asking to purchase or feu about seven poles of ground fronting Dundas Street for the erection of a Parish Hall. His request was declined.

However, Mr G.L. Dewhurst of Aberuchill had more success with his request to be allowed to take rabbits on his land on a portion of the railway between Comrie and Balquhidder. The Caledonian agreed so long as the rabbits were either trapped or snared - no shooting with guns was allowed in the vicinity of the railway in the interests of the train crews and passengers!

CRIEFF JUNCTION, CRIEFF
SINGLE LINE—BALQUHIDDER TO CRIEFF JUNCTION.—Tablet Stations.—

UP.

		1	2	3	4	4a	5	6	7	7a	8	9	10	11	12	13	14	15	16	17	18	19	20
		Pas.	GD'S	Ps.	C'TLE Clas B	C'TLE Clas B	Pas.	Pas.	Pas	Pas.	G'DS	G'DS	Pas.	Pas.	Pas.	Pas.	MIXD	Ps.	MIXD	Pas.	Pas.	Pas.	Pass.

M.	C.		a.m.	a.m.	a.m	a.m.	a.m.	a.m.	a.m.	a.m.	a.m.	p.m.	a.m	p.m.	p.m.	p.m.	p.m.	p.m	p.m	p.m.	p.m.		p.m.
—	—	Balquhidder dep.	7 5	7 40	...	...	...	...	8 30	...	1022	...	...	1220	2 15	...	3 15	...	...	4 30	...	...	7 0
2	2	Lochearn- { arr.	7 11	7 47	...	...	M O	...	8 36	...	1028	...	...	1226	2 21	...	3 21	...	4 37	S 50	...	...	7 6
		head...... } dep.	M O		...	6 15	C	...	8 38	...	1029	...	...	1228	...	...	5 22	...	4 42	...	...	...	7 7
9	27	St. Fillans { arr.	*		...	6 33	...	...	8 53	...	1044	...	...	1243	...	...	3 37	...	4 56	...	...	...	7 22
		{ dep.	6 35	7 10	...	7 45	8 55	...	1050	...	1145	1245	...	2 30	3 38	4 34	...	5 1	...	...	...	7 24	
15	18	Comrie ... { arr.	6 48	7 25	...	7 58	9 8	...	11 4	...	1159	1259	...	2 42	3 52	4 48	...	5 13	...	...	...	7 38	
		{ dep.	6 50	7 40	7 40	8 0	9 9	...	1112	...	1230	1 25	...	2 50	3 54	4 50	...	5 20	...	...	7 15	7 40	
21	7	**Crieff** ... { arr.	7 5	7 55	7 55	8 14	9 23	...	1127	...	1250	1 40	...	3	5	9 5	5	5 35	...	...	7 30	7 55	
		{ dep.	7 10	8 18	...	8 20	9 25	9 55	1143	12 0	1 15	1 40	...	3	3 4	14	5 22	...	6 28	6 35	7 32	8 0	
22	49	Highlandman ,,	...	7 14	F O	...	3 23	...	9 59	1146	1215	...	1 54	...	3 12	...	5 26	...	6 32	6 39	7 36	...	
25	49	Muthill ...... ,,	...	7 19	...	...	8 28	...	10 4	1150	1245	...	2 0	...	3 18	...	5 33	...	6 37	6 44	7 41	...	
27	50	Tullibardine ,,	...	7 24	...	...	8 34	...	1010	1154	1 5	...	2 6	...	3 23	...	5 39	...	6 43	6 49	7 47	...	
30	7	Crieff Jun....arr.	...	7 29	...	...	8 39	...	1015	1159	1 15	...	2 12	...	3 27	...	5 45	...	6 50	6 55	7 53	...	

	Arrives at	Gls g'w	P'th	F'th	Glas gow	Dun dee	Stir ling	Stir ling	B'ck ford	P'th			Lar- bert	Dun dee		Lar bert	Glas gow		Dun dee
	Destination	8 57	9 0.9	0 9	*45	1037	1055	1235	1 30	3 5			4 15	5 35		7 46	8 45		9 20

The speed of Trains passing over the banking at Edinchip Viaduct, between
The speed of Trains when passing round 12 or 13 chain curves, between

*No. 3—Starts from St. Fillans on Mondays only. Crosses No. 2
Down at Comrie.
No. 4a—Comrie must advise Crieff on Saturdays when this Train
is to be required. It will be worked by Engine, Brakesman, and Van
of 8.50 a.m. Cattle Train, Crieff to Perth, which will leave Crieff at
7.5 a.m. and arrive Comrie at 7.20 a.m.
No. 5—Crosses No. 5 Down at Crieff. * Arrives Glasgow 10.2 a.m.
during September.
No. 6—Crosses No. 5 Down at St. Fillans.
No. 7a—Crosses No. 7 Down at St. Fillans, No. 2 Down at Comrie.
and No. 11 Down at Muthill.
No. 9—Crosses No. 11 Down at Comrie.
No. 11—Crosses No. 12 Down at Comrie and No. 13 Down at Crieff.
No. 12—Does not call at Dalchonzie Platform. Crosses No. 16
Down at Crieff and 17 Down at Muthill.

No. 13—Crosses No. 16 Down at St. Fillans.
No. 15—Arrives Muthill 5.31 p.m. Crosses No. 19 Down at Muthill.
No. 17—Crosses No. 22 Down at Muthill.
Up Trains (except Nos. 12 and 20) call at Dalchonzie Platform to set
down Passengers on their intimating to the Station Master at St. Fillans
their desire to alight, and to take up Passengers on their intimating
to the Signalman at Dalchonzie at least 5 minutes before the Train is
due to leave St. Fillans.
Passengers travelling from St. Fillans to Dalchonzie must take out
Tickets to Comrie; Passengers joining the Train at Dalchonzie must
be pointed out by the Guard to the Station Master at Comrie, who will
issue Tickets specially provided for the purpose.
The Guard will collect the Tickets of Passengers alighting at Dalchonzie and hand them over to the Staff at Comrie.

AND BALQUHIDDER.
Balquhidder, Lochearnhead, St. Fillans, Comrie, Crieff, Highlandman, Muthill, Tullibardine, and Crieff Junction.

DOWN.

Dis- tance from Crieff Jun.			1	2 Exp Pas.	3	4	5	6	7	8	9	10	11	12	13	14	15	16	17	18	19	20	21	22	23
				G'DS F O	Pas.	Pa.	Pas.	Pas.	Mxd	G'DS	Exp. Pas. S O	Mxd	Pas	Exp Pas.	Ex. Pas.	Exp Pas.	Pa.	Ex. Pas.	Pa.	G'DS	Exp Pas.	Pa.	Pa.	Exp Pas.	M'd

M.	C.	Departs from	P'th ling	Stir ling				Dun dee ling	Stir ling	P'th	Dun dee		Stir ling	P'th	Dun dee b'ne	Glas gow		Dun dee	B'ck ford	Glas gow		Glas gow	s
			4 0	5 35				7 10	8 30	5		9 45		115	1220	11	11 10	pm	1 40	3 10	4 5		520	

			a.m.	a.m.	a.m	a.m.	a.m.	a.m.	a.m.	a.m.		a.m.	p.m.	p.m.	p.m.	p.m.	p.m.	p.m.	p.m.		p.m.	p.m.	
2	37	Crieff Jun....dep.	6	M O	8		9 8	...	...	11 0	1138	...	1 31	2 38	...	S O 3	5	30	5 24	...	6 5	8 15	
4	78	Tullibardine ,,	6 4		8 14		9 14	...	...	1144	...	1 36	2 43	...	3 11	3 45	5 28	...	611	6 33	8 27	
7	38	Muthill ,,	6 20		8 19		9 20	...	...	1150	...	1 41	3 37	...	317	5 55	5 34	...	617	6 37	8 27	
9	0	Highland- { arr.	6 25		8 25		9 25	...	...	1155	...	...	...	...	5 22	4 20	...	622	...	8 34	
		man { dep.	6 26		8 26		9 27	...	...	1157	...	1 46	2 43	...	324	4 20	5 sa	...	624	6 43	8 34	
9	0	**Crieff** { arr.	5 8		8 31	8 18	9 30	9 50	...	1122	12 0	1 49	2 45	...	2 55	324	2 55	41	550	631	6 50	8 38
14	69	Comrie { arr.	5 0 6	33	8 25		10 1	1030	10 55	...	12 3	1255	55	...	5 30	...	550	8 38
		{ dep.	5 06	33	8 25		1015	1045	...	...	1217	1 00	2	...	3 19	345	...	6 4	645	7	
		Comrie { dep.	5 20	66	8 39		1025	1122	1 7	...	1218	1 42	3	...	3 22	347	...	6 5	...	7	
20	60	St. Fillans { arr.	5 35	7 10	8 40		1035	1135	11 21	...	1231	2 8	20	...	36 34	2	...	617	...	7 20	
		{ dep.	5 45		8 55		1045	...	11 22	...	...	1 30	...	...	3 40	...	...	618	...	
28	5	Lochearn- { arr.	6		9		11 0	...	...	...	...	1 44	...	...	3 44	...	...	631	...	
		head— { dep.			7 20	8 9	9 9	11 8	...	1 7 38	...	1 46	...	250	3 50	...	...	632	...	
30	7	Balquhidder arr.			7 27	8 18	9 15	1115	...	11 45	...	257	4 3	...	...	638	...	

Balquhidder and Lochearnhead, must not exceed 10 miles an hour.
Crieff and Comrie, where there are guard rails must not exceed 12 miles an hour.

No. 2—Crieff Tickets collected at Muthill. Crosses No. 3 Up at Comrie.
No. 5—Crosses No. 5 Up at Crieff and No. 6 Up at St. Fillans.
No. 7—Conveys Merchandise for Lochearnhead and Balquhidder only.
Crosses No. 7a Up at St. Fillans.
*No. 8—Ceases after 31st August. Crosses No. 7a Up at Comrie.
† Will call at Comrie and Lochearnhead to pick up Passengers for
Loch-Awe and beyond.
No. 10—Crieff Tickets collected at Crieff Junction.
No. 11—Crosses No. 7a at Muthill and No. 9 Up at Comrie.
12—Crosses No. 10 Up at Comrie. No. 13—Crieff Tickets collected
at Muthill. Crosses No. 10 Up at Crieff. No. 14—Crieff Tickets
collected at Dunblane.
No. 16—Crosses No. 12 Up at Crieff and 13 Up at St. Fillans.
No. 17—Crosses No. 12 Up at Muthill.
No. 19—Crosses No. 14 at 5.32 p.m. Crosses No. 15 Up at Muthill.
Crieff Tickets collected at Muthill. Crosses at Highlandman on Satur-
days; Highlandman to collect Crieff Tickets of Passengers joining on
that day. Crieff to send a Man to Muthill by No. 15 Up to assist with
the collection of Tickets and help with Luggage as required.
No. 20—Empty Plant must not be sent by this Train unless

specially ordered.
No. 21—Must not be delayed more than 10 minutes for 5.10 p.m.
Train from Perth when this Train is running late.
*No. 22—Ceases after 31st August. Crosses No. 17 Up at Muthill.
No. 23—Only conveys Live Stock for Crieff as a Mixed Train. Must
not be delayed more than 20 minutes for 7.44 p.m. Train from
Perth, and not at all if that will not maintain the connection. Perth
will telegraph Crieff Junction whether or not there are Passengers for
Crieff Junction and Crieff Branch Stations travelling by the 7.44 p.m.,
and when there are, and the connection is missed, the Crieff Branch
Train will make a double trip.
Down Trains (except No. 9 and 13) call at Dalchonzie Platform to set
down Passengers on their intimating to the Station Master at Comrie
their desire to alight, and to take up Passengers on their
intimating to the Signalman at Dalchonzie at least 5 minutes before
the Train is due to leave Comrie.
Unless in possession of Tickets to St. Fillans, Passengers must be
booked from Comrie to St. Fillans.
The Guard will collect the Tickets of Passengers alighting at Dalchonzie, and hand them over to the Staff at St. Fillans.

Caledonian Railway Working Timetable for the line, 1907.

Chapter Ten

Traffic Operation on the Railway

The Working Timetable for 1906, the first full year of operation of the whole length of the line, shows the following trains running westwards to Comrie or beyond:

Goods train (Fridays only), leaving Perth at 4 am and arriving Lochearnhead at 6 am.
Passenger and Parcels train, leaving Stirling at 5.35 am and arriving St Fillans at 7.10 am.
Passenger train, leaving Lochearnhead at 8am and arriving Balquhidder at 8.07 am.
Passenger train (Mondays, Wednesdays and Saturdays only), leaving Dundee at 7.10 am and arriving Balquhidder at 9.10 am.
Passenger train leaving Perth at 9.05 am and arriving Balquhidder at 11.15 am.
Goods train leaving Crieff at 10.30 am and arriving St Fillans 11.15 am.
Passenger train leaving Gleneagles at 11.18 am and arriving Balquhidder at 12.35 pm.
Passenger train, leaving Lochearnhead at 2.50 pm and arriving Balquhidder at 2.57 pm.
Passenger train leaving Gleneagles at 3.05 pm and arriving St Fillans at 4.02 pm.
Passenger train leaving Glasgow Buchanan Street at 4.05 pm and arriving Balquhidder at 6.40 pm.
Passenger train leaving Gleneagles at 6.05 pm and arriving Comrie at 6.45 pm.

Eastbound trains were more varied:

Goods train leaving Balquhidder at 7.40 am and arriving Lochearnhead at 7.47 am.
Cattle train leaving Lochearnhead at 6.15 am and arriving Perth at 9 am.
Passenger train leaving Comrie at 6.50 am and arriving Stirling at 8.05 am.
Cattle train (Mondays only, and conditional on there being sufficient business) leaving Comrie at 7.40 am and arriving Crieff at 7.55 am.
Passenger train leaving St Fillans at 7.45 am and arriving Gleneagles at 10.02 am.
Passenger train leaving Balquhidder at 8.30 am and arriving Crieff 9.45 am.
Passenger train leaving Comrie at 10.15 am and arriving Crieff at 10.30 am.
Goods train leaving St Fillans at 11.25 am and arriving Perth at 3.05 pm.
Passenger train leaving Balquhidder at 12.45 pm and arriving Gleneagles 2.12 pm.
Passenger train leaving Balquhidder at 2.25 pm and arriving Lochearnhead 2.31 pm.
Mixed train (of passenger coaches and goods wagons) leaving Balquhidder at 3.15 pm and arriving St Fillans 3.43 pm.
Mixed train leaving St Fillans at 4.34 pm for Crieff where the goods wagons were detached. The train then continued to Gleneagles as a passenger train, arriving at 5.45 pm.
Mixed train leaving Balquhidder at 4.30 pm and arriving Crieff 5.35 pm.
Passenger train leaving Comrie at 7.15 pm and arriving Gleneagles 7.53 pm.
Passenger train leaving Balquhidder at 7 pm. On Mondays, Wednesdays and Saturdays it ran through to Dundee arriving 9.20 pm but on other days it terminated at Lochearnhead at 9.07 pm.

The working timetable also carried instructions to drivers not to exceed 10 mph when passing over the banking at Edinchip viaduct (probably whilst the earthworks were consolidating) and 12 mph when passing round the sharp curves on either side of the Thornhill tunnel.

The line was single track throughout from Crieff to Balquhidder with passing loops at the stations and was, of course, worked on the 'tablet' system whereby

An early postcard of St Fillans against a backdrop of Loch Earn.   *J. MacIntosh*

St Fillans station.   *J. MacIntosh*

a train was only allowed to continue on its journey if the driver had been given a 'tablet' by the signalman authorising him to proceed to the next station. The only signal boxes were located at the stations with the exception of Dalchonzie, which controlled both a level crossing and a refuge siding. This siding could only be used by up (eastbound) trains; the Working Timetable instructed that wagons destined for the siding on down trains had to be taken forward to St Fillans, shunted and returned in the up direction. Right up to the end of the line's operation, the signals were of the Caledonian lower-quadrant type.

At both Comrie and St Fillans the main station buildings were situated on the down platform with only a shelter and the signal box on the up platform. At Lochearnhead and Balquhidder the main buildings were on the island platforms.

Dalchonzie Halt appears to have had quite an interesting history. Not opened until 1903, a typescript note in the late J.F. McEwan's collection states that it was,

. . . a halt provided for the Lady owner of the estate and her tenants but ordinary passengers were allowed to use it 'if they appeared respectable or were tourists visiting within the area'. The station was designed by the Lady owner although an architect drew up the final building plans. The station structure had a private waiting room and the signalmen's cottages were in keeping with the design of the main building.

The Caledonian tried to encourage passengers to visit the new line by running a special Saturday afternoon express between Perth and Balquhidder and offering a cheap day return ticket of 1s. 6d. for the round trip of nearly 80 miles.

The locomotives employed on the ordinary services were usually McIntosh 0-4-4 tank engines of the '439' class with 0-6-0 tender engines ('Blue Jumbos') being used on the tri-weekly expresses.

The Working Timetable for the summer of 1907 showed an even better service and is reproduced in this book. These improvements included some trains starting their journeys from St Fillans instead of Comrie and continuing to Glasgow and Edinburgh or to Perth and Dundee. In the westbound direction a new express ran in July and August leaving Dundee (West) at 9.45 am and calling only at Magdalen Green (9.49 am), Perth (10.16-10.21 am), Crieff (10.50-10.55 am), St Fillans (11.21-11.22 am) and arriving at Balquhidder at 11.45 am where it made a connection with the 12.04 pm to Oban (2.26 pm arrival).

However, even this so-called 'express' took an inordinately long time to traverse the new route:

Dundee Magdalen Green-Perth   20.0 miles in 27 minutes = 44 mph average
Perth-Crieff   17.8 miles in 29 minutes = 37 mph average
Crieff-St Fillans   11.7 miles in 26 minutes = 27 mph average
St Fillans-Balquhidder   9.3 miles in 23 minutes = 24 mph average

The 21 miles between Crieff and Balquhidder therefore occupied 50 minutes. Stopping services generally took only slightly longer.

Crieff station with an eastbound train at the platform.   *J. MacIntosh*

McIntosh class '439' 0-4-4T No. 15159 takes water at the south end of Balquhidder station on 11th June, 1927.   *H.C. Casserley*

Passenger fares were, as always, a matter for public grievance. Two years earlier, in 1904, a deputation from local towns had met the General Manager of the Caledonian to complain about their exorbitant fares and had negotiated the following rates which were to be tried experimentally to see whether they would increase revenue:

Glasgow to Crieff, return: first class 11s. 11d., third class 5s. 10d., the latter down from 7s.
Glasgow to Comrie, return: first class 13s. 7d., third class 6s. 8d.
Glasgow to St Fillans, return: first class 15s. 3d., third class 7s. 6d.

The company also promised to look at ways of improving the frequency of the train service.

David Anderson, in an article on the railways of Crieff published in the July 1997 issue of *Steam Days*, analysed the Caledonian Railway's 1914 summer timetable which probably marked the high point of services on the line. Through passenger trains ran from Edinburgh (Princes Street) and Glasgow (Buchanan Street) to St Fillans via Gleneagles at third class return fares of 15s. 6d. and 11s. 11d. respectively. The Saturdays-only 'Strathearn Express' left Glasgow at 1.08 pm and Edinburgh at 1.00 pm, reaching Crieff at 2.35 pm although its onward journey to St Fillans did not arrive there until 4.45 pm. Eastbound the express left St Fillans at 7.40 am, arriving in Glasgow at 9.45 am and Edinburgh at 9.55 am.

Besides this express there were through coaches from Edinburgh (Princes Street) to Crieff at 9.25 am, 11.30 am, 1.25 pm, 4.25 pm (Saturdays only) and 4.50 pm (Saturdays excepted), From Glasgow (Buchanan Street) the through trains left at 10.10 am, 12 noon, 4.05 pm, 4.45 pm (Saturdays only) and 5.00 pm (Saturdays excepted).

The article goes on to say that, on average, there were three trains daily in each direction between Perth, Crieff and Balquhidder, all connecting at the latter station with trains on the Callander & Oban line.

There were great expectations of traffic being developed, especially in long-distance west-to-east freight and livestock trains between the Western Highlands and the eastern cities such as Perth, Dundee and the large industrial towns of Fife. There was even optimistic talk of ships from America using Oban as their arrival port on the west coast of Scotland and sending their cargoes by the new and shorter line.

But the anticipated traffic never materialised and the line sank into perpetual second-class status. As a wartime economy measure Lochearnhead station closed on 1st January, 1917 and did not re-open until 1st February, 1919. Traffic was lighter during the currency of the winter timetables and had been reduced during World War I but even at the time of the Grouping in 1923, when the Caledonian became part of the LMS, Crieff station handled around 20 passenger train movements every weekday. Twelve westbound trains ran from the main line at Gleneagles; of these three terminated at Crieff, two at Comrie, three at St Fillans and four (one of then Saturdays only) ran right through to Balquhidder. At the same time, four trains ran from Perth to Crieff where they connected with the westbound trains from Gleneagles whilst a fifth train ran right through from Perth to Balquhidder.

Ex-Caledonian Railway McIntosh '55' class 4-6-0 No. 14604 at Crieff on 29th July, 1936.

R.W. Kidner

Eastbound passenger train at Comrie *c*.1930, headed by a McIntosh 'Dunalastair III' class 4-4-0.

A. McGregor

In 1926 three trains from Gleneagles ran to Comrie, three more were extended to St Fillans and a further one ran through to Balquhidder. From Perth there were four weekday trains to Balquhidder and a fifth on Saturdays. Two of these trains ran non-stop from Perth to Crieff.

An unusual addition to the passenger traffic came in the late 1920s and early 1930s. In 1919 a wealthy Glasgow shipbuilder, William Gilchrist McBeth, had purchased the huge Dunira estate near Comrie as a wedding present for his son who subsequently inherited the business. The estate had become very run-down in the course of World War I and its economic aftermath, and when the Glasgow shipyards were themselves plunged into crisis after 1929, Mr McBeth ran a daily train packed with unemployed shipyard workers to Comrie to give them work on renovating various parts of his Dunira estate.

Once the Depression years were over, things improved with the increase in leisure travel in the 1930s. A Sunday-only service was instituted from Dundee to Oban which picked up at all stations except Dalchonzie Halt and during the summer months there were also half-day and evening excursions from Glasgow, Edinburgh and the industrial towns in the Forth-Clyde belt.

There were perennial complaints about the high level of fares and, just as today, it was the business commuter and standard ticket holder who suffered most. On the other hand there were excursion fares by special or ordinary service trains at fares that appear incredibly cheap. The following are a random selection from the weekly advertisements in the local Strathearn newspapers:

July 1906: A special train from Crieff to Wemyss Bay, departing at 7.30 am and arriving at 10.15 am, followed by a steamer trip through the Kyles of Bute to Rothesay. The return train departed Wemyss Bay at 5.29 pm and arrived Crieff at 8.15 pm. The fare was 4s. 6d. In the same year a daily excursion fare was on offer from Crieff and Comrie to Loch Awe by the regular service trains, including a cruise on the loch, for 5s. 6d.

February 1938: A special evening excursion train from Comrie (4.50 pm) and Crieff (5.05 pm) to Glasgow, returning at 10.40 pm. Fares 2s. 5d. from Comrie and 2s. 1d. from Crieff.

May 1938: The following fares were available by special excursion trains from Comrie:

St Fillans	7d.
Lochearnhead	10d.
Balquhidder	10d.
Perth	1s. 1d.
Dundee	1s. 7d.
Arbroath	2s. 1d.
Edinburgh	2s. 5d.

A trip to the Empire Exhibition in Glasgow by service train, including admission, cost 6s. 10d.

One of the best offers of 1938 was an excursion on Sunday 19th June from Crieff to Oban via Comrie (which must have reversed at Balquhidder Junction). The special left Crieff at 11.28 am and returned at 9.3 pm. The fare was 5s. 3d. from all stations to Balquhidder and both lunch on the outward journey and high tea on the return journey could be obtained at a cost of 2s. 9d. per meal including gratuities!

Looking east from Comrie station towards Crieff, *c.*1930.   *A. McGregor*

The signal box on the up platform at Comrie, *c.*1930 with John Robertson leaning out of the window. John Robertson retired in 1946 after 26 years as a signalman at Comrie, and 30 years railway service. A close inspection suggests that the box's interior was more like a horticultural shop than a working signal box!   *A. McGregor*

Station staff at Comrie, *c.*1930. *A. McGregor*

Station staff at Comrie, *c.*1930. *A. McGregor*

Comrie station looking west. The loading bank, goods shed and water tower can be seen in the yard on the left.   *A. McGregor*

Two members of staff, possibly shunters or fitters, at St Fillans *c.*1930   *A. McGregor*

Another 1938 bargain, which anticipated the post-war 'Runabout' tickets, was a Weekly Holiday Contract Ticket, valid for seven days, which encompassed various local areas. One example was a ticket covering the area Dundee-Perth-Stirling-Callander-Balquhidder-Crieff which was available for 13s. 3d. first class and 8s. third class.

A contemporary article by Robert D. Drummond titled '1935 Excursion to St Fillans' states that over the four-week period from 22nd June, 1935, no fewer than 24 excursion trains were scheduled to run to or through St Fillans. These trains originated as follows:

From Glasgow	6
From Dundee	6
From Edinburgh	4
From Aberdeen, Airdrie, Arbroath, Carluke	
Grangemouth, Kilmarnock, Leith and Stirling	1 from each

Four of these trains, all half-day excursions, had eventual destinations way beyond St Fillans but from all but one there was the opportunity to alight there and rejoin the train later in the day. Most of these trains would have been composed of corridor stock and would usually have included a dining car, making a heavy load over the severe gradients between Balquhidder and Comrie. Motive power for these trains would range from ex-Caledonian 4-4-0 and 4-6-0 types to Fowler 2-6-0 Moguls and double-heading would sometimes be necessary.

A number of the trains made a clockwise trip, usually out via Callander and returning via Crieff and Gleneagles. Some of them were termed Cruising Trains and their schedules allowed for them to run slowly between Callander and Crieff so that passengers could appreciate the superb views. These trains could each carry up to 500 tourists and were allowed a stop of up to two hours at St Fillans.

The 3rd July, 1935 was one of St Fillans' busiest days, when it received excursion trains from Arbroath, Stirling, Grangemouth and Airdrie.

World War II put an end to these excursions and the line never prospered in post-war years. It was now more convenient to travel by bus, coach or in your own motor car, and an increasing amount of cattle and freight traffic also transferred to road transport. Balquhidder engine shed was closed on 28th February, 1942 although the turntable remained in use for turning tender engines working on the line to Comrie and Crieff.

World War II did bring some extra traffic to the line in the form of trains bringing prisoners of war to the camps that had been set up at Comrie. One Sunday in November 1941 a series of seven special trains conveying the captured troops of Rommel's Afrika Korps arrived at Comrie. The POWs were detrained in the goods sidings, from where they were marched through the village to Cultybraggan Camp which had recently been constructed as a Prisoner of War Camp for hard-line German soldiers and Nazis.

Later in the war another POW camp was set up at Dalginross, on the southern outskirts of Comrie, to house Italian and lesser-risk German prisoners. These POW trains generally originated at the Channel ports; some were made up of

Balquhidder Junction in LMS days. On the right a train headed by a McIntosh 0-4-4 tank engine approaches from the Lochearnhead line whilst the Oban line curves away to the left of the picture. The engine shed, turntable and West signal box were situated in the 'V' formed by the junction. *National Railway Museum/LGRP 7956*

Member of staff, probably a guard, at Balquhidder *c.*1930. *A. McGregor*

An eastbound mixed train shuts off steam as it approaches Comrie across the Laggan Park in the 1930s, headed by a McIntosh class '439' 0-4-4 tank engine. The monument on the hill in the background commemorates Henry Dundas, Viscount Melville (1742-1811), a senior minister in the British Government who was known as the 'Uncrowned King of Scotland'. *W. Gardiner*

The fireman of McIntosh class '439' 0-4-4T No. 15216 takes his oilcan around the engine as it waits to leave Crieff with an eastbound train in LMS days. *R.M. Casserley Collection*

Pickersgill class '113' 4-4-0 No. 54476 waits to leave Crieff with the 12.30 pm from Perth to Balquhidder on 2nd June, 1951.   *H.C. Casserley*

Pickersgill class '113' No. 54476 being turned on the Balquhidder turntable in readiness for a return journey down the branch on 2nd June, 1951.   *H.C. Casserley*

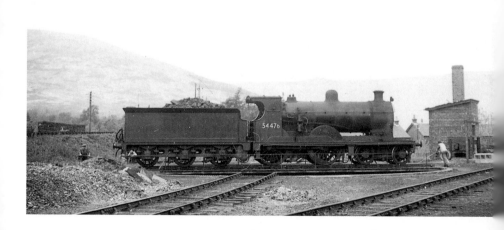

Southern Railway carriages painted in malachite green and others were made up of Great Western Railway carriages in chocolate-and-cream livery. They made an interesting change from the maroon livery of the LMS Railway's carriages that operated the routine service trains on the line.

The 1946 LMS timetable (*see page 132*) shows only two trains a day to Balquhidder, the first leaving Crieff at 8.12 am and arriving at 8.58 am, the second leaving Perth at 5.20 pm and arriving at 6.50 pm. In the other direction a train left Balquhidder at 9.17 am and divided at Crieff into a front portion which arrived Gleneagles at 10.26 am and a rear portion that arrived Perth at 10.57 am. A second train left Balquhidder at 7.40 pm and arrived Crieff at 8.23 pm. Although the journey time had been reduced to around 45 minutes, an average speed of only 28 mph made the railway extremely vulnerable to road buses.

The 7.36 am from St Fillans still ran through to Edinburgh but the return train in the afternoon only ran as far as Crieff, arriving at 6.43 pm and of no use whatsoever to any would-be rail commuters. Besides these trains, Comrie and St Fillans received another five trains per day - one from Crieff, one from Gleneagles and three from Perth and returned two to Crieff and two to Gleneagles.

An article by George Robin titled 'Last Days of the Balquhidder - Comrie Line' describes the line in June 1950, its last full year of operation. He travelled from Balquhidder to Comrie behind No. M14476, an ex-Caledonian 4-4-0 designed by William Pickersgill in 1916. Its train comprised an ex-Caledonian non-gangwayed brake composite toilet vehicle and an ex-LMS wooden-bodied third class brake. On an earlier journey in 1936 he had travelled the line on an afternoon half-crown (2s. 6d.) 'cruising train' from Glasgow (Buchanan Street), out via Balquhidder and returning via Crieff, on an all-corridor coach train headed by ex-Highland Railway 4-6-0 No. 14768 *Clan Mackenzie*, surely a 'foreigner' on that line.

The article goes on to describe a conversation the author had with the station master at Comrie in which the latter was pessimistic about the line's future. He said that the line had been given a last chance to improve its revenue, otherwise it would shortly be closed, but what chance did it have of attracting more passengers when the local bus fares were around only one-third of the equivalent rail fare?

The station master's fears were well-founded and the line between Balquhidder Junction and Comrie was closed to passenger services on 1st October, 1951, as were passenger services between Crieff and Perth. Although regular freight services were also withdrawn, the Balquhidder line was used for a time by construction traffic for the hydro-electric board's Glen Lednock area water catchment system and it was not until around 1959 that the track was lifted and most steel bridges removed.

By 1953, after the lines between Balquhidder to Comrie and Crieff to Perth had been closed, the train service (*see page 132*) had deteriorated to one train per day from Comrie which left at 7.48 am with through carriages for both Glasgow (arr 9.53 am) and Edinburgh (arr 10.12 am). The return train left Edinburgh at 4.25 pm reaching Comrie at 6.57 pm, Glasgow passengers having had to catch

Balquhidder Junction on 15th September, 1950. The line to Oban curve away to the north-west and that to Crieff runs off to the right. In the centre a Pickersgill class '72' 4-4-0 No. 54501 shunts the stock of a train from Perth alongside the West signal box.   *H.D. Bowtell*

Pickersgill class '72' 4-4-0 No. 54501 rests at Balquhidder after bringing in a train from Perth via Crieff on 15th September, 1950.   *H.D. Bowtell*

a separate train at 4 pm and wait for almost an hour at Crieff. Even in those days, the journey to both cities could be done by car in less than half the time.

By the time of the last full summer timetable service in 1963, Crieff was served by 10 railbus passenger trains from Gleneagles but only two of these continued onwards to Comrie. This service was totally inadequate and the end came only a year later.

No records appear to exist regarding the earliest motive power and rolling stock used on the line but the first train to arrive at Comrie in 1893 was hauled by one of Benjamin Connor's 2-4-0 engines, No. 467, and appears to have comprised an assortment of 6-wheeled carriages. In Caledonian days the local passenger trains were generally handled by the McIntosh 0-4-4 tank engines of class '439' which were introduced in 1900 whilst the heavier trains were provided with his 'Blue Jumbo' 0-6-0 tender engines. Traffic in the 1920s was generally handled by 0-6-0 goods engines, ex-Caledonian Railway 4-4-0 tender engines and 0-4-4 tank engines which were still to be found on the shorter runs; the range of motive power also widened to include ex-Midland Railway 4-4-0 3-cylinder compounds. Later still, Stanier 'Black Five' 4-6-0s and Riddles BR Standard class '4' 2-6-4Ts were to be found working the service to Comrie as well as the railbuses which were introduced on the line in 1958: more about them later.

The earthworks and structures on the line between Crieff and Balquhidder were of substantial construction with the intention of carrying heavy traffic. The only locomotives that the LMS prohibited from using it were their 'Jubilee', 'Patriot' and 'Royal Scot' class 4-6-0s and their 'Princess' and 'Duchess' class 4-6-2s. Even their large 2-8-0 tender engines were allowed on the line although they were not to run east of Crieff.

The locomotives working the regular service trains were generally based at Perth South (63A) or Stirling (63B) depots although one operated from the sub-shed at Crieff. There were actually two small sheds built side by side to the east of the station, relics of the time in the 1860s when the Crieff Junction Railway and the Crieff & Methven Railway built their separate lines to the town. Both buildings survived into the post-Nationalisation years but even the larger shed, which remained in use until the end of steam working in the area, was only just big enough to house a 20th century locomotive.

The carriages used on the local trains were generally older non-corridor stock that had been 'cascaded' down from more prestigious services, although the through coaches to and from Glasgow and Edinburgh were generally of better quality. It was rare to find a local train longer than three carriages; two or even one coach was the norm in later years. In the early days of the line there was no such thing as steam heating in the compartments and foot warmers were available at Crieff and Comrie stations.

The Appendix to the 1906 Working Timetable mentions all five stations on the line as having facilities for loading and unloading horses and private carriages. This was a very necessary provision as it was usual in those days for families coming to the district for their summer holidays, or for the grouse-shooting season, to bring with them mountains of luggage and a bevy of domestic servants as well as their private means of transport. Well-to-do

With Glen Turret in the background, Stanier 'Black Five' No. 44796, allocated to Perth South shed, approaches Crieff from the Comrie direction c.1960.

families would rent villas for an entire month or more, and a list of visitors to the area and their whereabouts was published in the weekly newspapers.

To complement these facilities the railway company advertised its passenger train parcel delivery service to local tradesmen. Crieff offered three daily deliveries plus two deliveries of perishable goods, all delivered free within a mile of the station. At Comrie the deliveries of ordinary goods were made at 10.30 am and 3.30 pm and of perishables at 8.30 am and 6.30 pm, again free with a mile of the station, whilst St Fillans delivered twice a day free to anywhere in the village.

All the stations on the line had quite extensive goods yards. Livestock formed an important part of the traffic in this area, particularly cattle which were sometimes transhipped south for slaughter and sometimes for wintering in more sheltered pastures. Through livestock traffic between the Western Highlands and Islands and the markets of Dundee would also travel by this route, with the train reversing direction at Balquhidder Junction. At Comrie, Colonel Williamson built a 'model' slaughterhouse adjacent to the station.

Other freight traffic, apart from general merchandise, included stone and slate from local quarries, timber from the various estates along the line, and lime for fertiliser products. In the reverse direction, coal from the Fife and Lanarkshire coalfields was an important import to fuel the house fires in the expanding villages along the length of Upper Strathearn. Comrie also handled a good number of horses that were taken to nearby Glen Artney for 'breaking-in'.

The line itself does not appear to have caused the Civil Engineering Department many problems. The Comrie-Balquhidder section in particular had heavy earthworks on a generous scale and the engineers had confined the concrete bridge spans to a maximum span of only 40 ft and used steel spans to bridge anything wider. This was much more conservative than 'Concrete Bob' McAlpine's viaducts on the Fort William-Mallaig line which was built around the same time; he constructed his Glenfinnan viaduct with 50 ft spans. However, in the first few months of 1903 there was severe flooding on the track between Monzievaird and Comrie. The banks of the River Earn were carried away near the Milton Burn and water rose to the level of carriage footboards. On 7th February the drivers of the 4.05 pm from Glasgow and the 4.25 pm from Edinburgh were warned of the danger but both managed to get through safely to Comrie.

The riverbank was not repaired promptly and, 17 days later, considerable damage was caused to the track half a mile east of Comrie station. Around 25 yards of ballast was washed away, leaving the rails and sleepers dangling over a torrent estimated to be four or five feet deep. Around 100 yards of the line near Comrie station was also under around two feet of water. A train from the south left Crieff around 3.30 pm but when it reached the breach the passengers had to dismount and walk across fields to the main road. The line was repaired overnight by a large gang of men in a ballast train.

Further west, about 50 yards before St Fillans station, water came down the hillside with tremendous force and washed away the ballast and formation to a depth of around five feet.

In March the Caledonian raised the level of the embankment by two feet for a considerable distance either side of the Milton Burn but this proved

Crieff station looking west towards Comrie, with a two-coach empty stock train at the eastbound platform. The former terminal station, now a goods depot, is on the left of the picture.
J.F. McEwan Collection, courtesy of Dunbartonshire Information & Archives

The engine sheds of the Crieff Junction Railway (opened in 1856) and the Crieff & Methven Railway (opened in 1858) standing side by side on the east of Crieff on 30th August, 1952.
R.M. Casserley Collection

Comrie station, possibly in the 1930s. The signal in the distance is a Caledonian Railway lower quadrant type. *J.F. McEwan Collection, courtesy of Dunbartonshire Information & Archives*

Permanent Way gang at Comrie in the 1950s. *Left to right*: A. Cameron, D. McLaren, J. Miller, W. Kean and P. McDuff. *George Miller*

Dalchonzie Halt in May 1956, looking east towards Comrie. The signal box controlled the level crossing gates and access to a nearby siding.
J.F. McEwan Collection, courtesy of Dunbartonshire Information & Archives

St Fillans station in May 1956. The line had been closed to passenger traffic for five years but the station and track are still in good condition.
J.F. McEwan Collection, courtesy of Dunbartonshire Information & Archives

The derelict Lochearnhead station in May 1956, looking east. The westbound track on the right of the platform has been lifted but the eastbound line is still *in situ*.
J.F. McEwan Collection, courtesy Dunbartonshire Information Archives

Balquhidder station looking towards Oban on 2nd June, 1951. The sign on the down platform says 'Change here for Lochearnhead, St. Fillans and Comrie' and the branch train waits at the island platform but not for very much longer: the line closed to passenger traffic only four months later. *H.C. Casserley*

insufficient. In that exceptionally wet year of 1903 flooding occurred again at that same point in both August and September.

Apart from this disruption, the line appears not to have caused any major problems and in times of heavy winter snowfalls, particularly those in 1895, 1900, 1947 and 1963, it was very often the only means of communication between Crieff and Comrie. In the last week of February 1947 the line was blocked between Crieff and Gleneagles on three occasions but was cleared within a few hours by the Perth snowplough, whilst the line between Perth, Crieff and Balquhidder was kept open throughout. By comparison the main A85 road was blocked between Crieff and Perth for almost a week.

The passengers on the line ranged from businessmen who lived in Upper Strathearn but with offices as far afield as Glasgow and Edinburgh, schoolchildren attending secondary school in Crieff or the world-famous Morrison's Academy, tourists and market-day shoppers. The line was also given a boost in 1940 when the children and teachers from Cargilfield School in Edinburgh were evacuated to Comrie and took up residence in Lawers House, Colonel Williamson's former home. Their journeys home to see their families, and vice versa, brought additional traffic to the line, as did the evacuation of 460 children and teachers from St Theresa's School in Glasgow who were brought to the district in 1940. Less willing passengers on the line during World War II were several trainloads of German and Italian prisoners-of-war bound for the camps that had been set up in the vicinity of Comrie.

Unfortunately, as the 20th century progressed, all these clients began to desert the railway for road transport or their own cars and tended to use the railway only when the roads were blocked by snow.

The railway has now been closed for so long that there are not too many people alive today with personal memories of the line. Luckily the author has received letters from some of them and their stories are recounted below.

Erlend McNab, as well as remembering the POW trains made up of coaches from all the Big Four constituent companies, also remembers an interesting newcomer to the line in the late 1940s in the form of a Gresley 'V1' class 2-6-2 tank engine or its development, the 'V3', which sometimes worked the early morning train to Balquhidder. This memory is shared by Christopher Grant who was a boarder at Cargilfield school from 1942 to 1946 when it had temporarily relocated to Lawers House and who made several journeys between Comrie and Crieff behind this engine on its return trip. No-one remembers its number but there were at this time two of these engines allocated to Stirling MPD: No. 67650 (a 'V1') and No. 67675 (a 'V3'). Maybe it was one of these, but what was it doing on CR territory?

One person who does have a vivid memory of the line is Ross Munro of Comrie who attended Morrison's Academy in Crieff in the late 1940s and, one summer Saturday in 1949, travelled with his school cricket team for a match against George Herriot's School in Edinburgh. The team boarded the train at Crieff and stowed their cricket gear in the rear van. Unfortunately for them, the train divided at Stirling into separate Edinburgh and Glasgow portions; the team continued happily on their way to Edinburgh whilst their equipment was last seen heading in the direction of Glasgow!

Jack Scott Miller moved to Pittachar, near Crieff, in 1934 and has memories of the boys from Morrison's Academy there being let out of school in time to catch the 'Comrie Express'; this may have been in winter time when the road was frequently blocked by snowdrifts. He also remembers wartime troop trains carrying sailors direct from Aberdeen to Oban and of specials carrying Italian prisoners of war to Comrie. His father used to buy cattle from Oban and they always arrived safely next day by rail. On one occasion, when his cattle wagons were being shunted at Tullibardine (between Crieff and Gleneagles) an altercation arose between his gardener and the engine's fireman which resulted in the latter pelting the gardener with coal. No doubt the gardener accepted the free gift with gratitude! Another memory was that the fireman working the last train of the evening from Gleneagles to Crieff would very often clean out the engine's firebox *en route*, with the result that the wooden trackside fences had to be renewed quite frequently.

Jack also recalls an occasion when the lady booking clerk at Highlandman station (near Crieff) was asked for a ticket to Crewe. In Jack's own words, 'She searched through the comprehensive ticket dispenser which showed such items as "Highlandman to Muthill", "Highlandman to Crieff with a dog or golf clubs", Highlandman to Gleneagles", etc., but could find no mention of Crewe. She finally said to the hopeful traveller, "We dinnae sell tickets to they oot o' the way places!".'

During World War II many local women worked on the railway and one of these was Ann (Nan) Rutherford Miller of Comrie who became a signalwoman at Comrie station. Her niece Carol Miller remembers one day in the spring of 1945 when Nan inadvertently pulled the wrong points lever during shunting operations in the goods yard and sent an engine down a short bufferless stretch of track to its fate in the mud. Manpower was short so it was decided to muster a party of German prisoners of war from the camp at Dalginross to assist the Perth breakdown gang in getting the engine back onto the rails. (This camp catered for German and Italian prisoners considered not to be dangerous, unlike the other camp a mile away at Cultybraggan which housed hard-line Nazis who even executed one of their own number in the camp for suspected collaboration with the Allies.)

The German gang arrived at the goods yard and, under the supervision of British guards, began trying to dig out the engine under Nan's direction. She shouted instructions from the signal box and gesticulated with her hands and fingers to indicate what they should do. Unfortunately she accompanied one verbal instruction with an indication comprising two fingers and the Germans immediately 'downed tools', protesting that her actions were insulting and in breach of the Geneva Convention!

The first moves to close the lines came in 1945, soon after the end of the war, when the LMS conducted an internal review of its train services in the Highlands.

Word soon leaked out and in October that year a Strathearn Railway Committee was formed to fight any proposal to close the Crieff to Balquhidder line. Public meetings were held in Crieff and Comrie and the help of both the County Council and the local MP was enlisted in its campaign to save the rail service.

The committee held a number of meetings with the LMS authorities who first of all denied that the review was taking place, then 'stonewalled' further

Table 338 PERTH, METHVEN JUNCTION, CRIEFF, and BALQUHIDDER

Miles			Week Days only a.m	a.m	am	a.m	p.m	p.m S	p.m E	p.m E	p.m	p.m	p.m	p.m	p.m K	p.m S
		Perth (General) dep	..	..	..	9 30	12 30	..	..	4 17	..	5 20	TC from Edinburgh (Table 285)	..	Commences 5th June	9 35
3		Ruthven Road	..	..	..	9 37	12B37	..	..	..	..	..		..		9 42
4		Almondbank	..	..	..	9 40	2 40	..	..	4 27	..	5 30		..		9 45
5		Tibbermuir	..	..	..	9 43	12B43	..	..	4 30	..	5 33		..		9 48
6½		Methven Junction	..	..	..	9H47	12H47	..	..	4H34	..	5H37		..		9H52
9		Balgowan	..	..	..	9 52	12 52	..	..	4 39	..	5 42		..		9 57
11½		Madderty	..	..	..	9 56	12 56	..	..	4 43	..	5 46		..		10 1
13½		Abercairny	..	..	..	10 0	1 0	..	..	4 47	..	5 50		..		10 5
15¾		Innerpeffray	..	..	..	10 6	1 6	..	..	4 54	..	5 57		..		1011
17¾		Crieff arr	..	..	..	1010	1 10	..	..	4 58	..	6 1		..		1015
—	Mls	Gleneagles dep	6 35	..	840	1120	..	3 0	3 0	Daily commencing 1st July	5 25	..	6 20	7 35	9 5	..
—	2½	Tullibardine	6 41	..	846	1126	..	3 6	3 6		..	..	6 26	7B40	9 11	..
—	5	Muthill	6 47	..	852	1132	..	3 12	3 12		5 34	..	6 32	7 44	9 17	..
—	7½	Highlandman	..	..	859	1139	..	3 19	3 19		5A41	..	6 39	7A50	9 24	..
—	9	Crieff arr	6 57	..	9 3	1143	..	3 23	3 23		5 45	..	6 43	7 54	9 28	..
—		Crieff dep	..	8 12	..	1148	1 12	3 25	3 35		..	6 5	..	7F56	..	..
23¾		Comrie ¶	..	8 24	..	12 0	1 24	3 37	3 47		..	6 17	..	8F 8	..	..
29½		St. Fillans	..	8 37	..	1213	1 37	3 50	4 0		..	6 30	..	..	..	..
37		Lochearnhead	..	8 51	..	..	..	..	..		..	6 44	..	..	..	..
39		Balquhidder arr	..	8 58	..	..	..	..	..		..	6 50	..	..	..	..

Miles		Week Days only a.m	a.m	a.m	p.m	p.m	p.m S	p.m	p.m	p.m	p.m	pm	p.m S	p.m	p.m K
	Balquhidder dep	..	..	9 17	..	..	..	..	..	..	..	740	..	..	..
2	Lochearnhead	..	..	9 21	..	..	..	..	..	..	..	744	..	..	..
9½	St. Fillans §	7 36	..	9 35	..	1225	..	1 50	..	4 55	..	758	..	..	..
15¼	Comrie	7 48	..	9 47	..	1237	..	2 2	..	5 7	..	810	..	..	..
21¼	Crieff arr	8 1	..	10 1	..	1250	..	2 15	..	5 20	..	823	..	..	..
—	Crieff dep	8 8	..	10 5	12 5	..	..	2 25	3 40	5 25	..	..	..	7 0	8 39
22¾	Highlandman	8J12	..	10 9	12 9	..	..	..	3 44	5 29	..	..	..	7 4	..
25¼	Muthill	8 17	..	10 14	1214	..	..	2 34	3 49	5 37	..	..	..	7 10	8 48
27¾	Tullibardine	8 22	..	10 20	1220	..	..	..	3 55	5 43	..	..	..	..	..
30¼	Gleneagles arr	8 28	..	10 26	1226	..	..	2 44	4 1	5 49	..	..	..	7 20	8 58
—	Crieff dep	TC to Edinburgh (Table 285)	8 5	10 18	..	..	1 52	..	Commences 1st July	..	6 5	..	8 27	..	Commences 5th June
23¼	Innerpeffray		8 9	10 22	..	..	1 56	..		..	6 10	..	8 31	..	
25½	Abercairny		8 13	10 26	..	..	2 0	..		..	6 14	..	8 35	..	
27½	Madderty		8 17	10 30	..	..	2 4	..		..	6 19	..	8 39	..	
30	Balgowan		8 21	10 34	..	..	2 8	..		..	6 24	..	8 43	..	
32½	Methven Junction		8H26	10H39	..	..	2H13	..		..	..	..	8H48	..	
34	Tibbermuir		8 29	10U42	..	..	2U16	..		..	6U32	..	..	..	
35	Almondbank		8 32	10 45	..	..	2 19	..		..	6 36	..	8 54	..	
36	Ruthven Road		8U35	10U48	..	..	2U22	..		..	..	..	..	..	
39	Perth (General) arr		8 45	10 57	..	..	2 32	..		..	6 46	..	9 4	..	

A Calls to set down from Glasgow or Edinburgh on giving notice at Gleneagles

B Calls to set down on notice at previous *stopping* station

E Except Saturdays

F Runs to Comrie only to take forward passengers from Gleneagles or beyond on notice at Gleneagles.

H Calls to set down on notice at previous *stopping* station and to take up on notice at Methven Junction

J Calls on notice to take up for Larbert or beyond

K Wednesdays and Saturdays.

S or S Saturdays only

U Calls on notice to take up

¶ Trains call at Dalchonzie Platform between Comrie and St. Fillans on notice at Comrie, also to take up on notice at Dalchonzie at least 5 mins. before train leaves Comrie. Heavy luggage or bicycles will not be dealt with at Dalchonzie

§ Trains call at Dalchonzie Platform between St. Fillans and Comrie on notice at St. Fillans, also to take up on notice at Dalchonzie at least 5 mins. before train leaves St. Fillans. Heavy luggage or bicycles will not be dealt with at Dalchonzie

LMS timetable for the line, 1946.

Bradshaw's Railway Guide, August 1953.

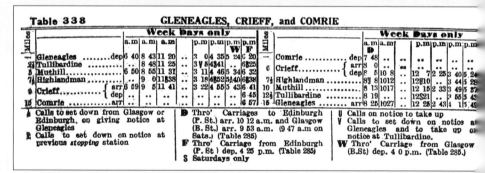

Table 338 GLENEAGLES, CRIEFF, and COMRIE

Miles		Week Days only a.m	a.m	a.m		p.m	p.m	p.m W	p.m F
—	Gleneagles dep	6 40	8 43	11 20	..	3 0	4 35	5 24	6 20
2½	Tullibardine	..	8 48	11 25	..	3V 5	4B41	..	6B25
5	Muthill	6 50	8 55	11 31	..	3 11	4 46	5 34	6 32
7½	Highlandman	..	9 0	11B38	..	3 18	4B52	5A40	6B38
9	Crieff arr	6 59	9 5	11 41	..	3 22	4 55	5 43	6 41
	Crieff dep	..	..	..	..	..	..	..	6 45
15	Comrie arr	..	..	..	..	..	..	..	6 57

Miles		Week Days only a.m D	a.m		p.m	p.m	p.m	p.m
—	Comrie dep	7 48	..	..	..	..	..	..
6	Crieff arr	8 0	..	..	..	..	..	..
	Crieff dep	8 5	10 8	..	12 7	2 25	3 40	5 24
7½	Highlandman	8U 8	1012	..	12U10	..	3 44	5 28
10	Muthill	8 13	1017	..	12 15	2 33	3 49	5 37
12½	Tullibardine	8 19	..	..	12S21	..	3 55	5 43
15	Gleneagles arr	8 25	1027	..	12 25	2 43	4 1	5 49

A Calls to set down from Glasgow or Edinburgh, on giving notice at Gleneagles

B Calls to set down on notice at previous *stopping* station

D Thro' Carriages to Edinburgh (P. St.) arr. 10 12 a.m. and Glasgow (B. St.) arr. 9 53 a.m. (9 47 a.m on Sats.) (Table 285)

F Thro' Carriage from Edinburgh (P. St) dep. 4 25 p.m. (Table 285)

S Saturdays only

U Calls on notice to take up

V Calls to set down on notice at Gleneagles and to take up on notice at Tullibardine.

W Thro' Carriage from Glasgow (B.St) dep. 4 0 p.m. (Table 285.)

A bird's eye view of a train on Lochearnhead viaduct and the line snaking its way along the side of Loch Earn, seen from the window of an Oban-bound train as it climbed Glen Ogle on 2nd June, 1951. *H.C. Casserley*

Comrie station with ex-Caledonian Railway 4-4-0 No. 54500 on a Gleneagles train in July 1958. The locomotive was one of the class '72' designed by William Pickersgill in 1920 and, at the time of the photograph, was allocated to Crieff MPD (63A). *National Railway Museum/REAL 3810*

Crieff station with '4F' class 0-6-0 No. 44193 on a Gleneagles train in July 1955. The locomotive was built by the LMS in 1924 to a Midland Railway design and, in 1955, was allocated to Crieff MPD (63A).   *National Railway Museum/REAL 2666*

Super-power for the branch train! The 12.30 pm Perth-Balquhidder two-coach train arrived at Crieff double-headed by Fowler '4F' class 0-6-0 No. 44251 and Pickersgill class '113' 4-4-0 No. 54476 on 2nd June, 1951. The pilot engine was detached here.   *H.C. Casserley*

questions for several weeks. Eventually they announced that they would not be closing any Highland lines and that the 1946 summer timetable would run a service of around 75 per cent of the pre-war level. However, a service that gave Lochearnhead and Balquhidder only two trains a day in each direction was hardly likely to entice many passengers onto the route, even though St Fillans, Comrie and Crieff did manage a few more trains.

The LMS and its successor, British Railways Scottish Region, kept the loss-making lines under constant review and in 1951 they announced that the lines between Balquhidder-Comrie and Crieff-Perth would close to passenger traffic on 1st October, 1951. The remaining section between Comrie and Gleneagles survived for another 13 years, worked by a variety of motive power with a load of only one or two coaches. The triangle of sidings in the Comrie goods yard, that had enabled tender engines to change their direction of travel in the days when the line terminated there, had been taken out many years previously and this now gave rise to a considerable amount of tender-first running between Comrie and Gleneagles. There was still a turntable at Crieff but it couldn't accommodate anything larger than an ex-Midland Railway 4-4-0 compound. Moreover, as there were no coaling facilities at Crieff, engines could only take on coal at Perth and it became common to see large engines such as Stanier 'Black Fives' hauling one or two-coach trains on the branch because they could operate all day without re-coaling.

In 1958, in an attempt to revive flagging passenger traffic, British Railways introduced railbuses onto a number of secondary lines in Scotland. These were built by the firm of D. Wickham & Co. Ltd. of Ware, Hertfordshire, and cost £11,000 each. These four-wheel vehicles incorporated the maker's normal method of tubular body construction which had rubber suspension between body and underframe, a Meadows six-cylinder horizontal diesel engine derated to 105 bph, radius arm-controlled axleboxes, air brakes and other features which resulted in a tare weight of 11½ tons for each 44-seat vehicle. Their maximum speed was around 60 mph.

The power unit rating was lower than on the firm's other railbuses and on test runs it showed a fuel consumption of approximately 9 mpg. Principal dimensions were:

Overall Length:	39 ft 10 in.
Length over body:	38 ft 0 in.
Width over body:	9 ft 0 in.
Overall height:	12 ft 7 in.
Wheelbase:	19 ft 0 in.
Wheel diameter:	2 ft 9 in.
Fuel Tank Capacity:	50 gallons

A cab was arranged at each end of the vehicle on the left hand side. The sliding aluminium doors opened into the central vestibule and were air-operated, controlled by a push-button on the driver's desk. Retractable steps with inside operating gear were fitted and transverse seating was arranged to face the cab at each end, with triple and double seats on either side of the gangway. An additional tip-up seat was positioned by the cab.

THE NEW
DIESEL RAILBUS

between

GLENEAGLES—CRIEFF—COMRIE

WEEK-DAYS—15th SEPTEMBER, 1958 to 14th JUNE, 1959
(or until further notice)

GLENEAGLES — CRIEFF — COMRIE

	Steam am	am	arr	an.	pm	pm	pm	pm	pm	pm	pm
Gleneagles.............lve	6 45	—	8 50	11 0	1 0	2 10	3 27	4 48	6 5	7 27	8 33
Tullibardine .... ,,	—	—	8 55	11 5	1 5	2 15	—	4 53	—	7 32	—
Muthill..................,,	6 55	—	9 2	11 11	1 11	2 21	3 36	4 59	6 14	7 38	8 42
Strageath Halt ... ,,	—	—	9 6	11 16	1 16	2 26	—	5 4	—	7 43	—
Highlandman .... ,,	—	—	9 8	11 18	1 18	2 28	3 42	5 6	—	7 45	8 49
Pittenzie Halt ... ,,	—	—	9 10	11 20	1 20	2 30	—	5 8	6 21	7 47	—
Crieff ....arr	7 4	—	9 12	11 22	1 22	2 32	3 46	5 10	6 23	7 49	8 53
,, ...lve	—	7 25	9 13	—	—	—	—	—	6 24	—	—
Comrie ....arr	—	7 37	9 25	—	—	—	—	—	6 36	—	—

COMRIE — CRIEFF — GLENEAGLES

	am	am	noon	pm	pm	pm	pm	pm	pm	Sat. only pm
Comrie ....lve	7 45	9 40	—	—	—	—	—	6 45	—	—
Crieff ....arr	7 57	9 52	—	—	—	—	—	6 57	—	—
,, ...lve	7 58	9 53	12 0	1 30	2 45	3 51	5 20	6 58	7 55	9 0
Pittenzie Halt ....arr	8 0	9 55	12 2p	1 32	2 47	—	5 22	—	7 57	9 2
Highlandman ....,,	8 2	9 57	12 4	1 34	2 49	3 55	5 24	—	7 59	9 4
Strageath Halt ....,,	8 4	9 59	12 6	1 36	2 51	—	5 26	—	8 1	9 6
Muthill ....,,	8 7	10 2	12 9	1 39	2 54	3 59	5 29	7 4	8 4	9 9
Tullibardine ....,,	8 15	10 10	12 17	1 47	3 2	4 7	5 37	—	8 12	9 17
Gleneagles ....,,	8 21	10 16	12 23	1 53	3 8	4 13	5 43	7 15	8 18	9 23

NOTICE AS TO CONDITIONS.—Tickets are issued subject to the British Transport Commission's published Regulations and Conditions applicable to British Railways exhibited at their Stations or obtainable free of charge at station ticket offices.

TRAVEL BY THE MODERN RAILWAY

B.R. 35000—FK—September, 1958.   McCorquodale, Glasgow

A two-car diesel multiple unit at Crieff station with a Gleneagles-Crieff-Comrie service on 9th July, 1956.   *J.K. Dewar*

A Wickham railbus, No. 79979, approaches Crieff station in 1963 with a train from Gleneagles. These had been introduced onto the Crieff-Comrie line in 1958 in an effort to reduce costs and increase revenue but they were unreliable in service and the venture was not a success.

David Anderson

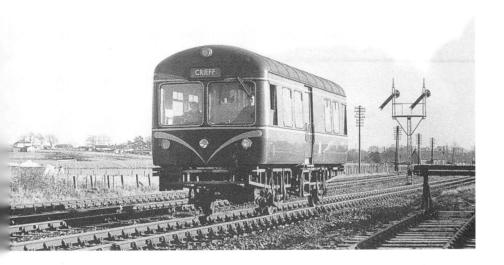

Comrie station and goods yard on 15th June, 1960 on the occasion of the SLS/RCTS Scottish railtour. Just visible under the station's footbridge is one of the preserved ex-CR carriages whilst the vehicle in the siding is a camping coach. *H.C. Casserley*

A view of Riddles BR Standard class '4' 2-6-4T No. 80063 on the last train to depart from Comrie, the 6.45 pm to Gleneagles on 4th July, 1964. *W.S. Sellar*

The first railbus to operate in Scotland went into service between Gleneagles, Crieff and Comrie in September 1958. It made 10 runs per day from Gleneagles to Crieff and back but only three of these were extended to Comrie. Tickets could be obtained from the guard on the train.

Unfortunately, these railbuses proved unreliable in service and breakdowns were frequent, especially in winter when a steam-hauled service would have to be substituted.

When Dr Richard Beeching published his 1963 report on 'The Reshaping of British Railways, it cited the Gleneagles-Crieff-Comrie line as an example of a service being so unprofitable that it did not even cover its own direct costs of operation.

The report said of it:

This is a rural service of 10 trains per day in each direction. There is an element of summer holiday traffic. The service is operated by diesel rail bus on weekdays only over a distance of 15 miles. Connections are made at Gleneagles with main line trains to and from Glasgow and Edinburgh.

Some 340,000 passenger miles accrue to this service which accounts for 65,000 train miles a year. On average, there are 5 passengers on a train at any one time. Earnings are £1,900 and these represent little more than a quarter of the train movement expenses of £7,500. Station terminal expenses bring the total of direct expenses to nearly £11,000, less than a fifth of what is covered by the earnings of the service. When track and signalling expenses are added - £8,200 - the total expenses are ten times as great as the earnings of the service.

Passengers using this service in combination with other services contribute more than £12,000 to the earnings of other rail services, and it is estimated that withdrawal of the service would result in the loss of £9,000 of this contributory revenue. Because there would be no alternative rail service on this line after withdrawal, none of the earnings on the service would be retained.

Despite the estimate of contributory loss, which is probably high, bearing in mind that holidaymakers may travel elsewhere, the overall net financial improvement expected from withdrawal is nearly £8,400, or more than two-fifths of the present level of total direct expenses attributable to the service.

Whatever one may think of the good Doctor's accounting logic, it appeared inevitable that the branch line would be one of its first casualties. So it proved, and the last train left Comrie for Gleneagles at 6.45 pm on the evening of 4th July, 1964, hauled by BR Standard class '4' 2-6-4T No. 80063. Later that evening the very last diesel service left Crieff for Gleneagles at 8.58 pm, driven by Bob McGuire, and the doors of Crieff station were locked for the very last time. The line's closure attracted little attention in the local press and there were no emotional farewells or 'last rites' performed. However the last train was given a rousing send-off from Crieff by Archie Fisher and the Kullions who had stayed over from a folk song concert the previous evening. Around 20 passengers were on board.

Graham Doig's father was a signalman at Crieff for the last five years of the line's existence and his mother was crossing keeper at Highlandman. He has supplied the following list of employees at Crieff station at the time of the line's closure:

Balquhidder station in May 1956 looking north-west. The Crieff line was closed to passenger traffic in 1951 but their trains had used the outer face of the island platform. Note the Caledonian Railway lower quadrant signal still in use on the up main line with the water column beyond it.
J.F. McEwan Collection, courtesy of Dunbartonshire Information & Archives

By the time this photograph was taken on 11th July, 1957 nature was beginning to take over the closed section of line west of Comrie where the railway crossed the River Lednock.
R.M. Casserley

Station master:	David Hay
Porters:	Danny Robertson, Sandy Don
Ticket Office:	Ian McMaster, Haig Gordon
Signalmen:	William Doig, Peter Comrie, and Wullie Elder
Railbus drivers:	Bob McGuire, Chic Robertson
Railbus guards:	Tommy Blair, John Watt

Within a few days contractors had ripped up the track and cut it into short sections to export to Japan as scrap steel. It may well have subsequently returned to this country in the form of motor cars.

A far cry indeed from 1890 when the passing of the Crieff & Comrie Railway Act was greeted with such wild enthusiasm in Comrie. A far cry also from 1893 when the railway was opened to Comrie and a banquet was held in honour of its main protagonist, Colonel Williamson.

Comrie had been served by rail for 71 years; the railway had opened and closed within the living memory of many of the inhabitants of the district. It was now regarded as an unwanted and unloved anachronism and people found it much more convenient to travel to Crieff by road.

Colonel Williamson had died over half a century earlier, in December 1913. On the day of his funeral the village came to a standstill for several hours and hundreds of people wound their way up to the family's private burial ground on the Lawers estate to pay their last respects as his funeral cortège passed.

It was very appropriate that on top of his coffin, lying on a large Union Jack alongside his sword and helmet, his wife placed a piece of the first turf of the Crieff & Comrie Railway that she had cut so many years earlier on that memorable day in February 1890.

The remains of Lochearnhead station looking towards Balquhidder on 7th October, 1967, 16 years after its closure to passengers. *R.M. Casserley Collection*

The masonry piers of the bridge across the River Turret at Crieff, 2003. The steel centre span has been removed.   *Author*

The approach to the west portal of Thornhill tunnel through a deep cutting, 2003. The public road was diverted away from the line at this point so that locomotives suddenly emerging from the tunnel would not startle horse-drawn traffic.   *Author*

Chapter Eleven

What is Left Today?

Early in 2004 the author walked over a large portion of what remains of the line between Crieff and Balquhidder. Readers wishing to do the same will find Ordnance Survey Landranger Maps 51 and 52, or even larger-scale maps, particularly useful

There is open public access to some parts of the line whilst other parts can be accessed by scrambling up and down embankments and cuttings, and very often making your way through dense undergrowth and quite mature trees. After all, it is now over half a century since the track was lifted between Balquhidder and Comrie and nearly 40 years in the case of Comrie to Crieff. In those days there was a big demand for scrap steel and those sections spanning the rivers were not left for long before being taken away for their scrap value, their stone or concrete abutments being left behind to gradually rot away. Fortunately for our story, these have not only proved wonderfully resilient but the concrete structures between Comrie and Balquhidder have weathered and blended well with the landscape, in the same way that the Glenfinnan viaduct is now regarded as a natural part of the West Highland landscape.

It is not always obvious what sections are private so would-be explorers are advised always to ask permission of wardens, etc., they may meet along their route.

Starting in the east, no trace whatsoever remains of Crieff station. Its site, immediately to the east of the King Street bridge, is now occupied by an ambulance station whilst the site of the adjacent goods station (the original terminal station) is now a health centre. The Station Hotel, prominent in photographs of the station, is still there but no longer offers accommodation to weary travellers and a supermarket has been built nearby on the site of the Town Meadow, to the west of the King Street bridge.

The tunnel beyond Burrell Street has been sealed but the high embankments on either side of the River Turret are still there. The substantial bridge over the river has lost its steel central section but the masonry arches still look impressive. The westernmost embankment, running parallel to Lady Mary's Walk, is still accessible to walkers.

Continuing westwards, there are no particular features on the line for the next couple of miles or so but its course can be seen in the distance from the south road from Crieff to Strowan. It can also be seen on foot at closer range from the Laggan Road which emerges close to the tunnel at Thornhill, on the now-diverted road away from Strowan House. Until the present A85 road was built as a turnpike road in 1804, this was the main road between Crieff and Comrie. It is now a public footpath but unauthorised vehicles are barred as it passes through now-private property; that is why the last two miles to Strowan are recommended to be traversed on foot. The tunnel itself, which is curved, is dry and solid underfoot but the cuttings on either side are overgrown.

From here the line's formation can best be seen from the A85 road into Comrie where the site of the station and goods yard have been totally

The road bridge carrying the A85 main road over the line by Comrie station, 2003. The station itself was situated immediately through the bridge but a caravan park has obliterated all traces.
Author

This is all that remained in 2003 of the huge concrete and steel viaduct over the River Earn at Comrie. This is were No. 123 and its special train are posing in the photograph on page 101.
Author

obliterated by a caravan park. The railway cottages are still standing on the wide approach road to the station and beyond them the visitor can appreciate the two sharp bends in the road which preserved Colonel Williamson's lime trees!

Immediately beyond the site of the station the line passed under the A85 and across a portion of the Laggan Park, bridging the River Lednock alongside the service road that was specially built to give access to Comrie House when the previous road was blocked by the railway embankment across Mill Lane. The layout has now reverted to pre-railway days, with Mill Lane (nowadays called Nurse's Lane) again giving access to Comrie House so those two bridges have been demolished. However, the nearby third bridge that carries the A85 over the river still stands and is a good example of the Caledonian's bowstring girder style; all three Lednock bridges were of this type.

The rising embankment at the back of the village, from the Lednock to Dundas Street and the crossing of the Earn, can still be traced although now largely built upon. Of the magnificent viaduct over the road and river (see the photograph of No. 123 proudly posing with the two saloons on the press run in 1901), there only remain the masonry abutments in Dunira Street next to the former East Free Church of 1866 (now a private residence) and two arches on the far side of the river. Unlike most of the other structures west of Comrie, their concrete piers are crumbling. Whether this is due to the weather or to damage caused when the steel span across the river was removed, the author cannot say.

A high embankment leads from these arches westwards on a falling gradient of 1 in 60 to road level in The Ross but it soon resumes its climb to cross the Earn for a second time. On the way, parallel to a public path known as the 'Sawdust Road', there remains a short section of track on which stands a private residence constructed from a goods wagon!

The second crossing of the Earn, at Tullybannocher, was on a very substantial concrete structure comprising several arches and a steel span over both the river and also the minor road from The Ross to Dalchonzie. The crossing span has been removed but the impressive concrete abutments remain.

The remains of the line as described above, from the crumbling arches near the Earn to the Tullybannocher crossing, can be seen by crossing into The Ross by the bridge on the A85 immediately west of Comrie. An Ordnance Survey map will be found very useful for finding your way around this area.

The next point of interest on the line is Dalchonzie Crossing where the minor road mentioned above joins the A85. Here the old signal box has been extended and converted into a private house but the track bed can be walked for some distance westward, crossing the Earn for the third time and passing through the ridge of rock that caused so much trouble to the railway builders.

The walkable section extends to within about half a mile of the final crossing of the Earn at Tynreoch. From this point the land is privately owned and the track bed is crossed by a gate bearing the ominous warning: 'Beware of the Bull'. On the occasion of the author's visit, the animal in question was standing menacingly in the adjacent field so railway research was temporarily abandoned in the interests of personal safety!

The remains of the bridge over the River Earn and Ross road at Tullybannocher, west of Comrie, 2003. *Author*

The former signal box at Dalchonzie Platform, now converted into a private house, 2003. *Author*

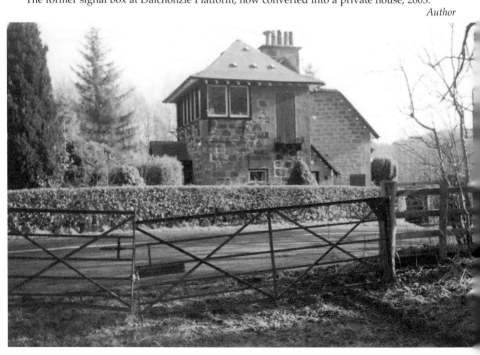

Retracing one's footsteps, the road journey on the A85 from Dalchonzie to Tynreoch is less than two miles. Parking near the latter is difficult but the railway's bowstring bridge can be seen, now carrying an estate road, down to the left as it crosses the Earn close to the A85 overbridge.

A little way further along the road to St Fillans there is a small rock outcrop on the north side of the railway. Around a century ago a group of local lads decided to paint these rocks in the form of a crocodile and this became a well-known feature of the line; so much so, in fact, that the Caledonian Railway itself used to maintain the paintwork so that the crocodile became a feature of the journey. Even today the crocodile is regularly repainted and has become a roadside feature pointed out to tourists by the railway's arch-enemy: the tour coach driver!

For the rest of the way to St Fillans the railway is on the right-hand side of the road and passes through Littleport farmstead before arriving at St Fillans station which is accessed via Station Road. At the time of writing, the 'Station Road' road sign was only visible from the further side of the right-hand turning from the main road; the explorer needs to keep a lookout for the station buildings which are visible on the hillside as the offices of a caravan site on the right of the A85.

In spite of its conversion into a caravan site, St Fillans station has been well preserved. The main station buildings on the down side are intact and both the platform buildings and the signal box survive on the up platform.

Immediately west of the station the roadbridge has been demolished and the embankment has been built upon by private houses, but a public footpath leads through a field from which it is possible to scramble up the embankment beyond the houses and subsequently walk through the 62 yds-long tunnel. The tunnel itself is quite dry but on the day of the author's visit the cutting on the far side was decidedly squelchy!

The track bed can be followed further westwards but several of the bridges over the many burns have been demolished, necessitating detours, and some of the land is now in private ownership.

The magnificent viaduct at Lochearnhead still stands, with no official public access although it appears to be possible to (unofficially) scramble up the western embankment at the Lochearnhead village/Glenogle end to gain access. A modern house at the eastern end of the viaduct blocks the way of anyone who crosses the viaduct from walking further eastwards towards St Fillans.

The bridge across the A84 at Lochearnhead has been demolished but the station immediately beyond it has hardly changed in a century!

Lochearnhead station was built in red brick with a signal box at the far end of the island platform and extensive sidings at the viaduct end; it also had a loop line next to the up platform line. Apart from losing its signal box and all its tracks, it is still instantly recognisable today from the photographs taken just before its opening day in 1904.

Today it is owned by the Hertfordshire Scouts who use it as a base for their outdoor activities. However, whilst the Scouts will always make visitors welcome, the reader who wishes to most savour the atmosphere should visit the station during the winter months when he can wander around the site alone with only the ghosts of the past for company. (This also applies to visits

The first major rock cutting on the line, west of Dalchonzie, 2003.   *Author*

The bridge over the River Earn and trackbed looking eastwards towards Dalchonzie, 2003.

Author

Side view of Dundurn viaduct, 2003. *Author*

The rock outcrop by the lineside near St Fillans, painted to resemble a crocodile's head, 2003.
Author

St Fillans station from the approach road, 2003. *Author*

St Fillans station from the east, 2003. A caravan park now occupies the site but most of the station buildings have survived and have been sympathetically cared for. *Author*

St Fillans station: the signal box on the up island platform as seen from the site of the goods yard, 2003. *Author*

St Fillans tunnel: the western approach through a rock cutting, 2003. *Author*

Lochearnhead viaduct: all that can be seen from the south side through the modern foliage, 2003!
Author

Lochearnhead station up platform with the site of the goods yard beyond it to the left, 2003. The station is now owned by the Hertfordshire Scouts. *Author*

Lochearnhead station: the former exit from the north end of the platform, 2003. It was originally completely enclosed by a wooden canopy like the the one shown on the postcard of Balquhidder station on the rear cover. *Author*

to St Fillans and Balquhidder, where the caravan sites are usually deserted in the winter months apart from their wardens.)

Continuing onwards from Lochearnhead, now in a southerly direction and climbing steeply for two miles to make a connection with the Callander & Oban line, the final engineering feature of the line is the magnificent viaduct over the Channdroma burn at Edinchip. Here the river valley is spanned by three lofty concrete spans on one bank and two on the other. The central steel span over the river, long ago removed for scrap, has now been replaced by a narrower span which continues a cycleway all the way from Callander to Killin and utilises in part the track beds of both our own railway and the former Callander & Oban lines.

Access to the cycleway can be gained at either Lochearnhead or just south of the Edinchip viaduct. From there to Balquhidder our railway crossed the line of the modern A84 until it made a junction a short distance further south with the Callander & Oban at Balquhidder Junction.

In its heyday Balquhidder Junction was a significant place on the railway map. Its significance and size have already been described in previous chapters but today it has been almost completely obliterated by a caravan site.

Driving along the A84 between Callander and Lochearnhead, its location is marked in both directions by roadsigns saying 'Balquhidder Station'.

The only remains of the station are a subway that used to lead from the road to the island platform and a flight of steps that used to lead onto the down platform; this was used by trains between Glasgow/Callander and Oban. Just beyond the steps are the remains of the brick-built passenger shelter on the down platform.

All that now remains of Balquhidder station as seen from the A84 road in 2003. *Author*

The remains of the subway entrance to Balquhidder station on the A84 road in 2003. *Author*

This concludes the description of the lines in 2004. But what of the buildings in Comrie, which their owners decorated so enthusiastically to welcome the railway in 1893?

Almost without exception, the buildings still stand today, albeit sometimes under different ownerships. The Ancaster Arms has been rebuilt to convert the hotel bedrooms into private apartments and the Commercial Hotel is no longer used for that purpose. Most of the shops mentioned still remain as shops but are now owned by different proprietors.

Happily, the ceremonial spade and white kid gloves used by Mrs Williamson when cutting the first turf of the Crieff & Comrie Railway have survived, as have the illuminated Address and set of silver bowls presented to the Colonel at his testimonial dinner. All are in private hands and are lovingly cared for by their owners.

And so ends the story of the railways of Upper Strathearn. They have come and gone within little more than half a century. Effectively, they started as the personal ambition of one man, Colonel Williamson, to benefit the village of Comrie. They extended, again partly through Colonel Williamson's efforts, to benefit St Fillans, Lochearnhead and Balquhidder. But, in the end, both privately-formed companies had to sell out to the mighty Caledonian Railway in order to see their dreams fulfilled.

The viaduct at Edinchip, between Lochearnhead and Balquhidder, in 2003. The original 80 ft steel central span (visible on the left of the photograph) was removed for scrap after the line closed but has recently been replaced with a narrow-width steel span so that the viaduct now forms part of a long-distance cycleway. *Author*

Appendix

The Crieff and Comrie Railway
An Ode by Sidney Herbert Willby

An ode entitled 'The Crieff and Comrie Railway' was written by Sidney Herbert Willby to celebrate the cutting of the first turf of the railway on 13th February, 1890. Willby appears to have been a younger contemporary of William McGonagall, 'poet and tragedian of Dundee', who was a master of bathetic verse and had the reputation of being the world's worst poet. The reader can judge for himself whether Willby runs him a close second.

In tones of gentle sweetness blend
The lyric and the lay,
The spirits of the 'Stephensons'
Are in our midst today!
The fire of this achievement adds
A lustre to the flame
That gilds such deeds with glory in
The golden globe of Fame.
Brim up the clinking glasses, and
Let wine and music flow!
When wanes the fight 'tis meet and right
To quaff the fallen foe.
Let torches stream, and gala gleam,
Let banners brightly wave,
And lustily ring forth your cheers
In honour of the brave!
None but the stalwart victors know
The fury of the fight,
Nor e'en gauge the vastness of
The foeman's subtle might.
But they have fought and conquered,
Have rent the foeman's mail,
And gained twixt Crieff and Comrie
The mighty Iron Rail.

The purple heath, the golden corn,
The sunny-tinted glade
E'er long will see their beauty shorn
Beneath the worker's spade.
The creaking crane, the hammers ring,
The anvil's merry sound,
Anon will ding where songsters sing
In Flora's bright abode,
Soon stately staunch the Iron-king
Will roam his Iron Road.
The lady who this august day
Displac'd the verdant earth,
Hath crown'd the victors of the fray!
A Railway given birth!!
Perchance sweet Admiration's gaze
Imbued with Fancy's flame,
May ask who wear the crowns of praise,
List! I will give them name.

The foremost is a soldier who,
In Lawr's the lovely dwells,
A man beloved as good and true
And who, a whisper tells,
Once wander'd far o'er Egypt's plains
When strife and war were rife,
Unheeding princely perils, pains,
Unmindful of his life.
The gallant Briton wing'd his ride
Far o'er the sandy wave,
Nor tarried till he knelt beside
A Scottish soldier's grave!
Serenely soft the setting sun
Gleam'd glory o'er the head
Of noble Colonel WILLIAMSON
Returning with the dead.

When twilight rays of amber light
Beam'd bright on Moredun's breast,
A poet, drinking deep delight,
A shepherd thus addresst:
Who dwells in yon majestic hall,
Where hale the heather grows?
Where voices soft in cadence fall,
And blooms the blushing rose?
And soon the rustic shepherd said,
In accents rich and rare,
Hast thou in histr'y never read
Of those who tarried there?

Look you at yonder battlement
Declining in decay,
Whose sable stones still represent
Bright ages pass'd away.
The foeman falter'd, feign'd, and fell
Beneath its sire's steel,
Where now the dwellers' actions tell
The pride the peasants feel.
Believe me, sir, my kinsmen true,
And e'en the very leaf,
Give Honour's golden greeting to
Sir ROBERT D. MONCRIEFFE.

Now favour on another falls,
Full firm in mind and will,
Whose voice once rang in 'Senate Halls',
And should resound there still:
By beautiful Blair Drummond,
And wide of silver Tay,
The hearts of maid and man respond
To Colonel D. MORAY.

Where circles Cowden's floral dress,
And glow-worms glitter light,
There lives a touch of tenderness,
A thrill of true delight.
M'NAUGHTON, bold as chieftain mail'd,
Peace be within thy home!
O'er Life's rough sea thy barque has sail'd,
In safely plough'd its foam.
'Remembrance will thy form retain'
When Time unborn is dead, -
When Autumn leaves bedew'd with rain
Tell Manhood's Summer's sped.

Extending from this iron tree,
Four branches rich in leaf,
Portray in Talent's high degree
The skill that circles Crieff.
Oh! bonny Caledonia,
Ne'er will thy lustre wane
Whilst thou hast sons like these to stir
The hearts that love thy reign:
BROUGH, COMRIE, CRERAR, M'INTYRE,
Let no man dare gainsay
The incense which our thanks inspire
Ascend to thee this day.

Many a brilliant jewel gleams
In Perthshire's placid sky,
But calm and steadfastly there beams
A Light suspended high,
In pleasure pert, in duty grave,
Who e're his foes defied,
His soul is deep as Liten's wave,
As boundless as the tide.
Designers may the theme unmask,
In theory set the bones,
But oftentimes a greater task
Hath he who builds the stones.
His talents as a torrent teem
In this and other lands.
The structure of the Railway Scheme
Was fashion'd by his hands.
A toiler in the fields of Time,
A gem of commerce law,
The bells of admiration chime,
Their strains to D.N. SHAW.

In travels far o'er sea and land,
Full many men I've met,
But there is one among the band
My soul will ne'er forget.
An engineer by talent wrought,
A bard by Nature born,
His clear brain bristles bright with thought
Like 'Autumn Leaves' at morn.
His Lyrics, light of Love impart,
Truth twitters in their tale;
'The Power of Music' fills his heart
Like wind the spreading sail.

His pen 'Selina's' beauty drest,
Hath fashioned 'Youth in Age',
And tho' deep 'Darwin' reigns opprest,
Life sparkles in each page.
A crown of foster laurels wreathe
Thy brow, Admired YOUNG.
Ne'er will (whilst thou has't power to breathe)
The Harp remains unstrung.
The Signalman upon the line
May give the signal 'Clear',
And passengers in peace recline
Whilst YOUNG is Engineer!

Now, in the twilight of my lay
While sunset streams afar,
I would a modest tribute pay
Unto a Rising Star.
It sparkles in a legal sky,
Grows stronger in its flame,
Gains fulness like the ripen'd rye,
And DEMPSTER is its name.

One of the lamps from Comrie station, now privately owned in 2003.   *Author*

Index